Into the Glory

Glory is God's solution for the darkness covering the earth!

Greg Brown

Into the Glory

ISBN-13: 978-1512039269
ISBN-10: 1512039268

Copyright © 2015 by Greg Brown.
All rights reserved.

Cover & design by: Philip Brown
Editing by: Loraine Coleman
No part of this book may be reproduced, stored in a retrieval system or transmitted by any means without the written permission of the author.

King James Version
Scripture quotations marked "KJV" are taken from the Holy Bible, King James Version (Public Domain).

The Message
Scripture quotations marked "MSG" or "The Message" are taken from The Message. Copyright 1993, 1994, 1995, 1996, 2000, 2001, 2002. Used by permission of NavPress Publishing Group.
http://www.navpress.com/

New American Standard Bible
Scripture quotations marked "NASB" are taken from the New American Standard Bible®, Copyright © 1960, 1962, 1963, 1968, 1971, 1972, 1973, 1975, 1977, 1995 by The Lockman Foundation. Used by permission.
www.Lockman.org

New Living Translation
Scripture quotations marked (NLT) are taken from the Holy Bible, New Living Translation, copyright © 1996, 2004, 2007 by Tyndale House Foundation. Used by permission of Tyndale House Publishers, Inc., Carol Stream, Illinois 60188.
All rights reserved. http://www.newlivingtranslation.com/ http://www.tyndale.com

Table of Contents

ACKNOWLEDGEMENTS

FOREWORD by Rebecca Greenwood — 9

INTRODUCTION Enter the Glory Zone — 13

CHAPTER 1 The Emerging Season of Glory — 15

CHAPTER 2 How this New Season Began — 21

CHAPTER 3 The Father and the Glory — 25

CHAPTER 4 The Glory Baptism Outpouring — 33

CHAPTER 5 How to Explain Water Baptism — 39

CHAPTER 6 Baptism from a Hebrew Point of View — 47

CHAPTER 7 Baptism in the New Testament — 55

CHAPTER 8 The Baptism of Jesus — 63

CHAPTER 9 The Knowledge of the Glory — 75

CHAPTER 10 Word Studies about the Glory — 83

CHAPTER 11 Can We See the Glory? — 87

CHAPTER 12 Jesus Promised the Glory — 91

Other Books by

GREG BROWN

Navigating the Crisis

The 7 Laws of Breakthrough

Ministry Contact Information

SKYWAY CHURCH

14900 West Van Buren Street

Goodyear, AZ 85338

info@skywaychurch.com

www.skywaychurch.com

Acknowledgements

I thank God for all the wonderful people that he has brought together in a new and special way during this Season of Glory. The first person I want to thank is my wife Dawn. When the glory baptisms first started, she came into the water with me and something amazing started happening. I am grateful that we have co-labored together in worship, baptisms and ministry. I am thankful Father has blessed me with such a special wife. I want to thank all of our apostolic team, all of you who serve faithfully and help me do all the things we need to get done every single day. Thank you to all who have lovingly served all the people who come out every Monday night with prayer and love. Some have served at the altar and others getting people in and out of the baptism waters. The Lord has blessed us so much with all of you working side by side. I also want to thank all our ASCEND Int. Ministers. You have championed this glory move with me by being baptized in the glory and taking it out to your spheres of ministry. Finally, I thank the Skyway family. Thank you for your support and prayers as we take the gospel around the world.

Into the Glory

Foreword

The Glory River Explosion Conference is one gathering that will always hold a special place in my heart and be marked as a very significant ministry experience. I was honored to be invited as a speaker. I vividly remember being in my prayer room seeking the Lord for His direction of the messages to share. I felt a strong tangible presence of the glory of the Lord almost as if the prayers of those at Skyway Church were already preparing the way in intercession for the gathering. The truth is I am sometimes able to feel when intercession has occurred before I minister at an event, because I experience a special grace and ability for me to hear the Lord clearly many days before arriving. This particular evening, I felt this occurring in my prayer room. A tangible presence of God's glory has come and has been present since this time.

As you will read in this book, the Lord spoke to Apostle Greg Brown to begin the spiritual act of baptizing into this glory river those who had a desire and felt the leading of the Lord to do so. I heard the many resulting positive testimonies and watched a number of my friends being baptized in the glory on the live web stream. It was evident that there was a supernatural glory and anointing being released and imparted as people were immersed in the water. I witnessed individual following individual being greatly touched by the Lord and being what is termed "slain in the Spirit." Greg and Dawn, Greg's wife, would support them in the water as they encountered the Lord. When they would come up out of the water, they were different. Actually, different is not the best descriptive word to use, the more appropriate word is transformed. Where there was depression, joy was realized.

Where there was deliverance and freedom needed, it was manifested. And for many where healing was needed, the miracle transpired. I found myself wanting to experience this awesome presence of God's glory and His love.

Soon, I was invited by Greg to speak again at the church. I could not wait! My one request? "After I speak can I get baptized into the glory? Greg, will you and Dawn baptize me?" He agreed to do so. Soon the night for me to minister arrived. I was excited to share, but more excited to encounter the Father's glory in the water. Friends, I was not disappointed. God's glory enveloped me and I floated in that water with the help of Greg and Dawn Brown for a long time. The Lord refreshed me, spoke to me and released a new measure of His glory to me. He took me to a war room in the throne room of heaven and showed me all the nations He was calling me to. Since that encounter, I have received invitations to nations in which I have never ministered. I received invitations from nations that I have carried in intercession for many years. I have also seen an increase in the healings and signs and wonders in our ministry and increased anointing in prophetic words that the Lord speaks through me. I am busy. I travel nationally and internationally as a minister. When I got in the water that night, I needed to be revived and refreshed. And my heavenly Father totally refreshed every part of my mind, will and emotions.

I began seeking the Lord concerning the glory move of God that is unfolding. First, He led me to read 2 Kings 5 which shares the story of Naaman being healed of leprosy after being instructed by Elisha to dip in the Jordan seven times. In this Bible passage, we witness Naaman offended at the instruction given to him by Elisha, *"But Naaman became angry and went away and said to himself, 'Surely he could have come out, and stood and called on the name of the Lord his God, and waved his hand over the infected area, and taken away the leprosy'"* (2 Kings 5:11, MEV). The healing word spoken through Elisha was not what Naaman was expecting to hear. His servants approached him and wisely stated, *"My father, if the prophet had told you to do some great thing, would you not have done it? How much more when he said to you, 'Wash and be clean'"* (2 Kings 5: 13, MEV)? Naaman heard the counsel of his servants and dipped seven times in the Jordan and he was healed.

The second scripture the Lord led me to was found in John 5:2-4, *"Now in Jerusalem by the Sheep Gate there is a pool, which in Hebrew is called Bethesda, having five porches. In these lay a great crowd of invalids, blind, lame, and paralyzed, waiting for the moving of the water. For an angel went down at a certain time into the pool and stirred up the water. After the stirring of the water, whoever stepped in first was healed of whatever disease he had"* (MEV).

Why do I reference these Bible passages? Because some might be inquiring as to why the Lord would choose to be touching so many in the baptismal water? The truth is, sometimes God moves in ways that our human mind does not picture or in a manner we might not expect. One thing I have learned in my years of ministry is that we are to expect the unexpected. We are to allow God to move in new ways and not always think we will know how or what His movement will look like. His ways are not our ways. If Naaman can be healed in obedience by dipping in the Jordan seven times, could God not ask some to enter into the water again to experience His glory and healing touch? If an angel stirred the waters at the pool of Bethesda, could God not send an angel to stir the baptismal waters in Arizona and abroad? I believe the answer is yes!

Friends, I want to encourage each of you who are hungry and stirred as you read the pages of this book to come and experience God. Or invite those who are a part of this glory move to come to your church or region and bring the glory to you. This is the beauty of what God is doing. Those that have experienced the glory in the baptismal water are also bringing this to other locations, and others are experiencing God's glory touch. This is not about one church or one location. It is about God touching those who are hungry for more of Him and His glory with His incredible Father's heart of love which truly transforms.

In closing, the following are two prophetic words the Lord revealed to me concerning this move of God while at the Glory River Explosion gathering in October 2014 and again on December 8, 2014, the night I was baptized into the glory.

> "One thing I was seeing really clearly and even when we are talking and sharing today is that from the fire that is resting on Skyway it will go out across Arizona. I saw seven other fires. Seven other fires lit across the nation burning. Not even just lit but burning and blazing across the state in Arizona that will then spread to the nation. I wanted to share that with you that there's going to be seven other locations that are going to burn with this fire. It will go across all of Arizona into all regions. Let the fire fall!"

> "Hear me, the word will spread from here because of the signs and wonders and the healings in the physical, the healings in the mind, the healing in the emotions. The word will spread and they will hear to go to what is happening here in Arizona to be healed, to be set free and to receive an impartation to take the glory where God sends them. Pastor Greg, I just speak even on Wednesday night when you are sharing that there will be an explosion of the glory river that will flow at Global Spheres out through the webcast into the nations."

My prayer for you, friends, as you read this exceptional testimony of how God is moving through His glory to impact lives that your life will be transformed. Apostle Greg, thank you for your faithfulness to our Heavenly Father, the Church, the state of Arizona and the nations.

Rebecca Greenwood

Into the Glory

Introduction

Enter the Glory Zone

Isaiah 60:1-2 (NASB)
"Arise, shine; for your light has come, And the glory of the LORD has risen upon you. [2] "For behold, darkness will cover the earth And deep darkness the peoples; But the LORD will rise upon you And His glory will appear upon you.

We are entering into a new season of God right now. It is a season where God's glory is going to come to us in new ways. We are seeing the Lord wake us up from an old season of discouragement and restoring us with His glorious light. He is healing us, restoring us and shifting us into a new victorious realm. It is time to arise, stand up and move out from under the circumstances which have kept us in despair in this past season.

Glory is God's solution to deep or gross darkness. Glory is different than ability, gifts or anointing. It is a dynamic of God that he chooses to release at the appropriate time and this is such a time. The world is filled with darkness. It is covering the earth. There are problems with people, diseases and catastrophes facing our world like never before. Darkness is affecting our health, our families and our finances. While everyone is wondering what to do, it is important to know that God has a solution to the problems that we face. He wants to empower us to be victorious, so we can become glory carriers who bring solutions to all the realms of life we walk in. The Church is called to be the light of the world. If gross darkness is covering the people of the earth, we need to move into the realm where God's glory appears upon us.

We need to be ready to move when God moves in times and seasons. The reason He is shifting us is so we can be victorious over the cycles of darkness coming against us. If we are already experiencing everything we need, we would be overcoming the darkness of our day. Now God has already given us everything for life and godliness to be more than conquerors through Jesus Christ our Lord. The times and seasons of God are when we learn to access what Christ has appropriated and use these weapons of the kingdom for our lives to experience daily victory. The season we are now entering into is one in which God is releasing his glory upon us. With this in mind, it is time to get ready for something new to spring forth upon us. This is the mindset I have embraced in my journey with God.

As I began to prepare for God to shift me and those I lead into a new season of glory, we also moved into a new dimension of God while baptizing people. I was open to something new, but I did not expect what happened to happen the way it did. In this book I am sharing my testimony about how I came to expect the new emerging season. Next I will share how the Glory Baptisms began and the theology connected to what is transpiring. This is not a new and different baptism. I believe we are starting to experience the fullness of what God has promised to release through this ancient rite. Finally, I will share with you how to embrace the glory, understand the knowledge of the glory and how to impart it by living a life as a glory carrier. I pray that his glory will touch you as you read the book.

Greg Brown

Into the Glory

1

The Emerging Season of Glory

Have you ever thought you were created to be a part of something greater than you were currently experiencing? Have you ever wondered if you would ever experience the moves of God like those recorded in the Bible? Have you ever felt something was about to happen and you were looking expectantly for it to manifest before you? If you answer yes to these questions you are created for such a time as this.

This is a new season; it is a new day. This is the season for the glory of God to rise upon His people to receive new hope, new life and new power. Glory is being released for two key reasons. First, it is being released to allow us to be free from the darkness which is wrapping around our hearts and squeezing life out of us. It is also being released so we can provide new solutions which the world needs.

God is calling us out of the darkness so we can lead others out as well. It is not a time to be judgmental or condemning. The darkness surrounding the earth has created a hypercritical atmosphere. People are continually perched upon the edge of angry outbursts. Emotions are running hot and high. The children of God need to guard against a religious spirit that is released in this darkness. This spirit would try to convince us that condemning others is really taking a stand for righteousness.

Jesus, who is the true manifestation of God's glory, refused to be trapped by this religious spirit. He brought glory into the gross darkness of his time. Now He is calling us to do the same. He brought hope to the hopeless, those who were rejected by the religious yet trapped in the darkness. He brought life to those who could express faith for something better than their current situations. This is what glory truly looks like when it appears on God's children. Glory appears first upon us; then it is released through us.

This is the season to know God's love in a fresh and exciting way. God's love is inviting us to be set free from despair, depression and even depravity. It is a season to know God as a good and loving Father. Jesus said many things about his relationship with the Father while he was on the earth. This glory season is when we, God's children, will start experiencing a similar relationship with Abba Father, which literally interprets as, Daddy God. Entering the glory realm is entering into a life changing experience as blessed and accepted children of the Most High God.

It is a season to know our self in a new way. The last season of despair and depression has caused many to lose hope that they can experience anything better or be of help to others as well. We have heard many curses and accusations from other people and even the thoughts in our own minds.

God does not look at us like this. He sees us differently than the portrait painted by the artist of darkness. He sees us as loved children. He created us to bless us. He chose to form us at such a time as this so we could be his ambassadors and representatives on the earth today. This is why we desperately need to experience

God's glory. It is in his glory that we are changed. We need to see ourselves in a brand new light to break free from the negativity trying to hold us down.

Finally, it is time to see the Church in a brand new light. The Church is God's agent for expanding the Kingdom of God throughout the earth. We are the Bride of Christ, the Temple of the Living God. It is time to leave the chains of darkness which are trying to stamp out our light. It is not the time to show the world what we are against; it is time to let the world know that God loves them so much He sent His Son to break the darkness and set the captives free. It is time for a fresh season of glory to rest upon the Church.

Entering a New Season

> **Ecclesiastes 3:1 (MSG)**
> ¹ There's an opportune time to do things, a right time for everything on the earth:

God works in cycles and seasons. There is a time for everything in our lives. Knowing the opportune time to do something is essential. One of the things I have learned about entering a new season is that it takes new ideas, new power and new emotions to get out of the rut of the last season. If we already had everything it takes to get where we are supposed to go, we would be there. In reality, we get there through God's process in our lives and each season is a part of this process.

We are now entering into a *glory season*. The Bible says there is a glory that is associated with God. The Hebrew word for this is *Kabod*. It connects God's glory in all of creation. This includes the heavens, the earth and mankind. There is another word connected with glory and it is *Kabed*. I call this Hebrew word, the anti-glory. It is used about forty times in scripture but in a a negative sense always connected to man and not God. It means something is very heavy and weighs one down.

In this next season emerging in the earth, glory is going to be the focus. This will be talked about, sought after and given to either man or God. The people of God and the people of the world are going to be moving into glory encounters. I am watching this unfold right now, and it has been emerging into place and will fully emerge in the next few years.

In the times that Jesus walked the earth, the devil tried to deter him from his mission. He knew Jesus was on a mission to take back the dominion Adam had given over in the garden. The devil's strategy was to get Jesus to fall for the wrong *glory and worship the wrong source...*

> **Luke 4:5-8 (NASB)**
> ⁵ And he led Him up and showed Him all the kingdoms of the world in a moment of time. ⁶ And the devil said to Him, "I will give You all this domain and its glory; for it has been handed over to me, and I give it to whomever I wish. ⁷ "Therefore if You worship before me, it shall all be Yours." ⁸ Jesus answered him, "It is written, 'YOU SHALL WORSHIP THE LORD YOUR GOD AND SERVE HIM ONLY.'"

This worldly glory is connected to the exaltation of man and the pursuit of personal gain without God. Chasing a glory that will in the end produce enslavement to the god of this world and the pain he brings.

You see, there is a glory on this earth that is counterfeit to the glory of God. It can look so enticing that the devil thought Jesus would go after it. He did not, but many a man has and many will do so in the future. This glory or counterfeit glory is what the world is going to fall for in this next season. Glorious structures, people, economies and more. It will look so wonderful to possess, and the cost to have it is connected to whom you will worship.

Everyone will worship someone or something. Man was created to worship. It is in us. Have you ever awakened with a song inside of you? Most people have and it is a reflection of the way God made us. We were made to worship him and to serve him alone. We were created to be the reflection of *his glory*.

> **1 Corinthians 11:7 (NASB)**
> ⁷ For a man... he is the image and glory of God...

Genesis 1:26 (NASB)
²⁶ Then God said, "Let Us make man in Our image, according to Our likeness...

This is a season of *glory*. As this time emerges we will continue to see this word. It will be used in many different ways, because it is on the tip of everyone's tongue. Embracing the glory from heaven is essential for us all at this time. God wants us to emerge victorious. He will come to us in times of worship that will cause us to shine seven times brighter. His glory will give us wisdom and solutions that are beyond the natural man's abilities. Now is the time to rise up and shine as God's glory is being released into our lives.

Into the Glory 2

How This New Season Began

We had been through a difficult seven year season. I felt that it was a time for change to be released. Everyone was feeling the weight of the past but also a new level of expectation was starting to fill the air. It was time to start moving forward again. It was time to let go of the past and embrace something new from God. We weren't completely sure what it was that we were about to embrace, but we knew it had to be different.

You can't get to a new place with the old methods. The old is great for that which it was used beforehand, but it cannot be the vehicle of the new season. We had to get ready for God to do something new and fresh in us. I was studying the Bible with a fresh set of eyes. We were praying with a new level of expectation, and we were listening to hear what the Spirit was saying to the Church.

This is how it all started when we shifted into the Glory Season.

When it all began we were intentionally contending for the glory of God to be released among us. After hearing Chuck Pierce declare that a Glory Explosion is coming to Arizona, I felt called in my heart to champion this move. God had spoken to me a year earlier that I was to start gathering the apostolic leaders of the state for worship and strategy. Now this prophetic word seemed to be the piece of the puzzle that we all needed to embrace for God's purpose.

Here is the portion of what Chuck Pierce said that got me started contending to shift into a new season of God's glory. Chuck was speaking about an open vision he had of America in 2008. God was showing him each state and what would transpire in each state.

...And then I saw what looked like the Glory River coming in and every state had this Glory River. God spoke that His triumphant people would start gathering in a new way. And His triumphant people would keep gathering... in places where the Glory of God dwells so strong. When this movement hit one of those places, what would happen is they would come out seven times brighter because the glory was so strong in this meeting place. And the Lord showed me they would be forming.

...The State that surprised me the most, and I would have never seen from Heaven the way God showed me, was Arizona. It was the brightest State. It was the State with Glory...Arizona had the most incredible glory explosion of any state in America. The Spirit of God began to cover this state. The Glory began to cover this state. God said it would be the first state covered by His Glory... Arizona became the most vibrant God moving Glory realm piece of land in America. I am here to announce tonight that is what you are going to accelerate into, starting today in the next two years.
- Chuck Pierce, Chandler, AZ June 27, 2015

After Apostle Chuck shared this word, I began a biblical journey searching out all that the scriptures had to say about the glory of God. I wanted to have an explanation of the glory that was biblical and tangible. We had to be contending for something that is more than goose bumps and feeling good. There has to be a tangible expression of the glory which would cause everyone to stop and say, "This must be God." In this journey I have found over nineteen biblical expressions of how the glory can be made manifest in our midst.

We were seeking God's new outpouring more than a good message or a great sounding song. We have so many great messages and songs in the Church today, but we are still lacking the inner experience of God's power. We know about the glory. We pray about it and sing about it, but where is the real experience that is changing our lives? Our experience seemed to be less than all of our declarations. We were hungry and desperate for a fresh manifestation of God's glory.

That fall we hosted seven days of twenty-four hour prayer. During that time we invited Keith Luker who was traveling throughout Arizona with *The Feast of Fire*. Keith had heard Chuck's word for Arizona and started going throughout the state. We asked him to join with us. The first night was kind of slow, but we started out on a new journey to experience God's glory in a new way. Each night we gathered new momentum and before long we started seeing the miracles show up.

Miracles during the New Season

The miracles of God have been both internal healings of the heart and physical healings of the body. The healings of the body are some of the most extensive we have seen. They are all happening during this time we have become intentional about seeking God for the glory.

The first miracle was when the Lord's glory broke clinical depression off of one of our staff members who did pastoral counseling every day. I had seen in a vision people having their hearts restored like the battery in a cell phone being recharged. As I walked around watching people, I could see them connecting to the glory and their hearts were literally being charged by the glory. When I walked up to this dear pastor, the Lord said, "She needs a new battery; hers will not take a charge." With that word the miracle of joy began to overtake her. Now, this pastor would be the least likely to start laughing out loud. Once the joy of the Lord came upon her, she could not stop. I started sending other drained people over to her, and they would start laughing uncontrollably as well. It was an amazing morning.

Many of the miracles are happening during the worship without specific prayer, such as one man's miracle of hearing. Suddenly, we were being told that an ear which had been deaf for thirty-five years had been opened! Our dear brother had waited to go to his doctor and have it verified before he told us. God was performing miracles without us praying for them to happen. This is a wonderful dynamic of the glory being released to the Church in this hour of facing deep darkness!

This move is more than signs and wonders; it is a visitation of Abba Daddy God showing us how much he loves us. The hunger in the people is being met with demonstrations of love. The love of God is truly the testifying mark of this new season of glory.

Into the Glory

3

The Father and the Glory

The Glory Season which we are now entering into can also be recognized as *the Season of the Father.* It is interesting to trace the past major historical moves of God and to connect the person of the Godhead which is emphasized. It seems that in these seasons of emphasis those things in life that were difficult to access are now easily accessed. The things which took so much effort and prayer are now simply a word away. The key to making this easier is that we enter into a deeper realm of fellowship. The Greek word for fellowship is described as follows.

> *Koinōnia:* "a having in common (*koinos*), partnership which is recognized and enjoyed through sharing a common experience.
>
> Vine's Expository Dictionary of Old Testament and New Testament Words.

God has always wanted us to have fellowship with all three persons of the Godhead.

1 John 1:3 (NASB)
³ what we have seen and heard we proclaim to you also, so that you too may have fellowship with us; and indeed our fellowship is with the Father, and with His Son Jesus Christ.

2 Corinthians 13:14 (NASB)
¹⁴ The grace of the Lord Jesus Christ, and the love of God, and the fellowship of the Holy Spirit, be with you all.

It is clear that when the scriptures were written, a deep level of fellowship was normal in the early church. But as time has gone by, the traditions of men have erased our close fellowship. Relationship with God has been blocked by the rituals of men. God in His great mercy has reached out to us to restore us back into the rightful place of biblical fellowship.

Let's walk through Church history together and look at how this has unfolded in the past. Fellowship with Jesus was restored when a new revelation of salvation through faith was brought by Martin Luther in the year 1517. Martin Luther boldly taught that salvation was not earned by good deeds but was gained through personal faith alone in Jesus Christ.

This led to revivals in Europe which then moved to the birthing days of the United States. These revivals were powerful in bringing people to the saving knowledge of Jesus Christ. The early settlers in America wrote in their 1620 Mayflower Compact that this new land would be a shining city on a hill to the world referencing Matthew 5:14. The eighteenth century brought great Jesus revivals such as the Great Awakening with ministers like Jonathan Edwards and George Whitefield. The great revivals bringing people into fellowship or relationship with Jesus continued through the 1800s and 1900s. Billy Graham Crusades reached over 210 million people for Jesus! In all of these instances we see that once Martin Luther explained the biblical revelation of this personal fellowship with Jesus, all of us have had access to this biblical experience. It was always there, but it was not being experienced until it was restored.

In the 1900s, a new kind of fellowship or *shared experience* was about to be restored. The Azusa Street Revival, led by William J. Seymour, brought the focus on the individual believer having a personal experience with the person of the Holy Spirit. Through the Azusa Street Revival, people began to have encounters with Holy Spirit like those in the early Church. This included the spiritual gift of speaking in tongues as well as believing for great evangelism and kingdom expansion with signs, wonders and miracles. Believers were made aware of the Holy Spirit once again like those in the New Testament church.

This restoration move sparked the modern Pentecostal Movement in the United States. Ultimately this restoration of fellowship with Holy Spirit birthed the modern missionary movement. This movement was embraced by all parts of the Protestant Church even by those who did not accept the belief of speaking in tongues.

Again in the 1960s and 1970s, Christians were being awakened to the restoration of all the gifts of the Holy Spirit. In this continued work of restoring the fellowship or *common experience with Holy Spirit,* believers began to have New Testament power encounters that brought healing, miracles, speaking in tongues and more into the daily life of a modern day believer. This move of restoration transcended denominations and brought the Church into a new realm of unity. It also birthed many more missionary efforts. The kingdom of God continued to expand greatly with these two seasons of restoration now combined.

Now we are entering into the Glory Season. This move is clearly marked by a new fellowship with the Father. As I have witnessed in all the various signs and wonders which have taken place, it can all be connected to *fellowship with Abba Father.*

Jesus paid the price for us to gain entrance to the Father. The Holy Spirit is God who lives in us. But what of the Father? To some, God the Father is a far off person, unapproachable and distant. To others, He is waiting for us in Heaven but not involved in our lives right now. The scriptures are very clear to us regarding God the Father. He's much more than any of these things.

JESUS INTRODUCES THE FATHER

Until Jesus came, God was not usually referred to as Father or even considered a father. He was Yahweh. Basically the word means, "I am." The Hebrew people were forbidden from vocalizing the name Yahweh. So they would spell it YHWH. English speaking people put the vowels in it so that it would make sense to us. When you read the name "Lord" in the Old Testament, it's really a translation of Yahweh or Adonai. The translators used "Lord" because of the Jewish belief that one should not utter the name of Yahweh. A God whose name you are not even allowed to speak seems ominous, distant and frightening. This is very much the way most Christians view Father God to this very day.

When Jesus came to earth, He didn't refer to God as Yahweh. Jesus called him "Father". He referred to the Father sixty five times in Matthew, Mark and Luke. He then used this term an additional one hundred times in the gospel of John. This is a remarkable shift from all the other books of the Bible. It was this level of intimacy that Jesus was so adamant about that led to his crucifixion.

> **John 19:7 (KJV)**
> ⁷ The Jews answered him, We have a law, and by our law he ought to die, because he made himself the Son of God.

He truly introduced mankind to God as the Father: A person with whom we can have a relationship. Before Jesus, it was not possible. Jesus said,

> **John 14:6 (NASB)**
> "I am the way, and the truth, and the life; no one comes to the Father but through Me."

> **Mark 14:36 (KJV)**
> ³⁶ And he said, Abba, Father, all things *are* possible unto thee; take away this cup from me: nevertheless not what I will, but what thou wilt.

Before Jesus came we could not have this type of relationship with the Father. Now we can and even more. Jesus introduces us to *Abba*. This word is so intimate it actually translates to us today as *Daddy*. It is an Aramaic word of endearment that is used in families for children of all ages who have a real and loving relationship with their daddy. It was a word that was never used to describe God in any Hebrew writings. Suddenly Jesus has this amazing close fellowship with Father as *Abba*. Watch what happens for us after Jesus made this possible.

> **Romans 8:15 (NASB)**
> ¹⁵ For you have not received a spirit of slavery leading to fear again, but you have received a spirit of adoption as sons by which we cry out, "Abba! Father!"

Now we are encouraged by the Holy Scriptures to cry out to our *Abba Daddy God!* In fact, once Jesus introduced this word Abba which is also known as the Greek word, *Pater*, it is used over forty times in the New Testament.

Here is a key scripture that demonstrates the united fellowship of all three persons of the Godhead from when Jesus was baptized.

> **Matthew 3:13-17(NASB)**
> ¹³ Then Jesus arrived from Galilee at the Jordan coming to John, to be baptized by him. ¹⁴ But John tried to prevent Him, saying, "I have need to be baptized by You, and do You come to me?" ¹⁵ But Jesus answering said to him, "Permit it at this time; for in this way it is fitting for us to fulfill all righteousness." Then he *permitted Him. ¹⁶ After being baptized, Jesus came up immediately from the water; and behold, the heavens were opened,

> and [i]he saw the Spirit of God descending as a dove and [j]lighting on Him, ¹⁷ and behold, a voice out of the heavens said, "<u>This is [k]My beloved Son, in whom I am well-pleased.</u>"

The Great Three in One was there, all three entities at one time! And thus, the relationship between Jesus, the Son, and the Father is introduced. We are invited to have close relationship with all three.

The first time I found myself using this term of endearment *Daddy God*, I felt a resistance from the congregation while I was speaking. I know that check in the spirit that feels a wall is going up. I thought about it and prayed about it. Why would this word cause people to resist?

We live in a *fatherless generation*. Many have grown up without Father in the home. He was the one who left, abandoned and rejected them. Even when the father was present in the household, he may have been associated with being stern, quiet and unemotional. When we talk about God we don't connect Him to this earthly person. When I spoke about Abba Father, Daddy God, these painful connections created invisible walls because of past hurts in the lives of those listening.

This new season of Glory is filled with many testimonies of how people have had intimate encounters or fellowship with Abba, Daddy God. During the times in the baptismal waters I have found grown adults laying their heads on my chest as they are being ministered to by their loving Heavenly Father. I have seen both women and men burst into tears when I pronounce Abba's blessing over them. There is something so deep and important about having Father's blessing that words cannot describe. I can only relay that even those who do not think they need this are moved greatly when it happens.

We are all created to know the love of the Father. We are all created to experience the power of his blessing and acceptance in our lives. The world we live in has done so much to create the opposite. For the most part we fail to recognize the impact of this void. Suddenly while this glory move of fellowship with the Father is taking place, I see firsthand the significance of the emotional healing that is being experienced. Words cannot express what depth of love and healing is transpiring right now. I can only urge you to come into the glory and have this fresh fellowship that is readily available now.

ATTRIBUTES OF THE FATHER

So, who is the Father? What is He like? Here is a brief list of the many things we find in scripture to describe Him:

- Matthew 5:48 says He is *perfect*.
- Matthew 6:4 and 6:6 says He *rewards us*.
- Matthew 6:8 says He *knows what you need* before you ask.
- Matthew 6:9 says we need to direct our prayers to the Father. So, the Father *is listening*.
- Matthew 6:14 says the Father is one who forgives us. He is *forgiving*.
- Matthew 6:26 tells us that He is *our provider*.
- Matthew 10:29 tells us that His *eyes are always on us*.
- Matthew 16:27 tells us that the *Glory* belongs to the Father.
- John 17:22 The *Glory* of the Father *makes us one*.
- Matthew 18:14 tells us that the Father *doesn't want one person to perish*.
- Matthew 23:9 says that Father God is *truly our Father*.
- John 5:22 tells us that Father *does not judge us*.
- John 6:32 says the Father *gives true bread* to us.
- John 6:44 says that the Father draws us to Jesus.
- Acts 2:33 tells us that the Father is the one who *gives us the Holy Spirit*.
- Romans 1:7 – Father God *gives us peace and grace*.

- Romans 2:4 – His *kindness leads us to repentance*
- Romans 8:15 – The Father *adopts us*.
- 1 Corinthians 8:6 – It is only *through the Father that anything or anyone exists*.
- Galatians 1:1 – The Father is the one who *raised Jesus from the dead*.
- Ephesians 1:17 – He is the *Father of Glory*

These are just some attributes of the Father. This Season of Glory is all about the Father releasing his love to the sons and daughters in his family. We are moving into His identity and acceptance. These are crucial components I am seeing that are setting God's children free. This move is not more of the same thing that has been happening before. It is a new season and a new day. The glory realm is now open to have rich fellowship with the Father.

Into the Glory 4

The Glory Baptism Outpouring

As the glory services continued, after the first two weeks of continual meetings taking place, I heard the Lord speak these words. *"Open the ancient wells of baptism."* When I heard this I knew that I had received clear revelation about the power of God that is released when a person is scripturally baptized. I had gained this revelation when I first entered the ministry. I read in Church History about miracles and healings when people were baptized. It was during this early season of my ministry that I saw people really touched by God when I would baptize them. I have written teachings about this, and it is a part of our "baptism class" at our church. I knew the Lord wanted me to teach on this subject once again and for me to go back into the water and start baptizing people again.

I proceeded to once again teach what the bible says should occur when a person is baptized into Jesus. I told people that I would be baptizing on the next night, which was a Monday. Any who had not been baptized, or were baptized out of a religious duty and felt they should follow this key step of the Christian walk were invited to join me.

I had expectation in my heart that God was going to do a great work in the hearts of those who would come out. About four people let me know they were coming out to be baptized. First, I spoke about the key scriptural components of water baptism. I had some music playing through the sound system, and we worshipped in the presence of the Lord. I asked some of our ministers to pray for the people before they entered the baptism. The combination of the worship and the ministry teams releasing prophetic words over the people moved us into a new realm of glory.

The power of God was far greater than what I have ever witnessed in the baptistery. It was as if the baptismal had become a glory zone. As the night went along, people who had no intentions of being baptized were compelled to get baptized because of how powerfully the Spirit was moving. They had no change of clothes, no towel, and it did not matter. They were being transformed in the glory. We closed out the first evening. We told other people who were waiting to come back on the next night. One young lady volunteered to get the names of those who were being baptized, and we still are not sure of the original count. We started getting names on the next night, and by best count we had just under a hundred people baptized into this glory realm within the first two weeks. The lives were being changed. Word began to spread to friends and family. Miracles were taking place and people started coming in from across Arizona. Within a few weeks pastors, leaders and other hungry people were flying in from other states to be a part of what is going on with the Monday night Glory Baptisms.

I am writing about this for others to read and take with them wherever they might be traveling. This is a short explanation of how this all started and the theology of what transpires when we are baptized into Jesus Christ.

Miracles in the Glory Baptisms

Part of what created this early momentum which is still happening today is the amount of miracles taking place in this glory environment. One young girl who was in the first group being baptized had been a *cutter* at the age of nine. She was fifteen at the time of her baptism. She left the baptismal and went to the changing room. When she removed the wet robe, she saw all the scars from her past completely removed. Not only the invisible scars from her heart, I mean literally the physical scars on her arms disappeared! Praise God!

Other amazing testimonies have continued to come in, such as this one. This lady had slept in a chair for the past two years because of a herniated disk in her back. She came to be baptized in the glory, and God completely healed her. She slept in her bed for the first time after she was completely healed in the baptism waters. She is now filled with joy and gratitude because the mercy of God has restored her this way.

Another man whose hands had no feeling from a former issue had all feeling fully restored. He was so happy about the inner healing God did in his heart that he was not aware that his hands had been healed until the next day. Before his healing, he could touch a super-hot cup with his bare hands because he had no feeling. The next morning after his baptism, he grabbed a hot cup from the microwave and was shocked that he felt the heat and jerked his hand away. God had completely healed him!

The list of physical healings continued to grow each week, but this is not all. The inner healings of the hearts and minds are equally powerful. People are going places with the Lord when they get baptized that completely sets them free. One young adult man, Luis, was weeping with joy and laying his head on my chest during the baptism. Afterwards, I asked him what had transpired while it appeared he was *out in the Spirit*. He told me that he was walking in heaven and encountered a young man smiling at him who asked him, "Do you know who I am?" Luis said "No." He was asked the same question by him once again. Finally the young man said to him, "I am your older brother." This older brother had died at three days of age. Luis spoke to him in heaven. He discussed private family matters which in turn were shared with his family at a later time. When he went home and told them of this experience, great healing was released to his entire family. As amazing as it sounds, there have been six testimonies of people who have gone into heaven and had life changing encounters while being in the baptismal waters.

Along with physical healings and heavenly encounters there are more testimonies of God taking people into a place where he can heal them of past trauma and restore them. Most of these simply say that they have encounters of peace that is difficult for them to describe. Here is a testimony that came in from a pastor…

> *Last night I was baptized in the glory baptism. When I entered the water, I could feel God the Father's presence. The peace was great. As Pastor Greg began to pray for me. The colors I saw were beautiful. It was a brown background with gold lights in it. That's the best I can describe. As Pastor Greg pronounced God's love and blessing to me he disappeared and the Heavenly Father was there. Even writing this I'm crying. It was healing, cleansing and I felt so loved and complete. During that time the color was a beautiful blue like the sky on a clear day - peaceful. Then I don't know where I went. I know I was at great peace. Then it's like I woke up and honestly, I don't know why I shouted and laughed. It was startling. I really wanted to go back to the peace, but I can say today I can feel that peace. Praise the Holy Father.*
>
> *Pastor Loraine*

The testimonies continue to come in, and they all have a common thread. God's love was experienced in a new and life changing way. Areas of the heart which have been troubled are healed, and people are filled with a glory peace that exceeds what they have known before.

There are many more miracle testimonies from people who are experiencing healing while at our Glory River services but were not baptized. One lady brought her daughter to the service and told us of three pending heart surgeries. We prayed for the little girl. Later, we heard the report that during the first minor operation the doctor recognized that the other issues had been resolved. No more surgeries!

Another miracle happened at the hospital. Esther had suffered a stroke and was unable to walk while being hospitalized. The first portion of her miracle was that the original diagnosis after tests of a major stroke had been *downgraded* by the doctor after further review. There had been major prayer in between the two discussions with the doctor.

Next, I was discussing with Esther and her husband all the miracles taking place. I could feel the glory of God filling the hospital room. Esther then declared, "I am supposed to get up and walk!" I said, "Then do it!" She swung her legs out of the bed and started slowly walking. The more she walked, the better she walked. She walked twice around her room and then marched out the door to the nurse's station to tell them that Jesus had just healed her!

I was so excited I felt led to call five people on the phone. I was aware that each of these needed a fresh touch of God's glory. As I told them Esther's story each one experienced God's glory right over the phone. It was one of the craziest days I can remember. Praise God!

Finally, there is Karen's testimony. She was a very active and strong adult serving as a Chaplain in our church. She was hit with a respiratory virus which lasted over eight months. The doctors did not know what to do to help her. They tried many different medications after several tests. She finally was reduced to twenty percent oxygen intake in her lungs. She was gasping for air while attempting to speak. She had been prayed for by me and others over and over again. Nothing seemed to help.

She persevered and came to one of the Glory River nights. (Sometimes we stop short of our miracles because what used to work doesn't seem to be working anymore.) This time she immediately felt improved by at least fifty percent by her estimations. She then decided after witnessing the baptisms that she should be baptized. She was completely healed immediately the night she was baptized. She also received a new glory impartation of healing. She has been praying for as many sick people as she can. She keeps giving the glory away, and it keeps growing stronger in her life. Karen moved into a new season by allowing God to do a new thing inside of her. There was a very profound inner healing that happened in the baptism waters. She refused to be stuck in an old season.

I share all of this with you to let you know that the glory of God is being poured out on us in different ways. The ones who are choosing to go into the glory baptisms are doing so because they feel that there is something God has for them in this step. Some are receiving in the water while others are receiving the glory in services or even hospitals or on the phone!

However you are moved by reading about the glory of God, please respond in faith. Let God do something *new* in you. Don't pre-suppose that you are going to get more of how God has already moved in your life. Get ready for something you have not received. This is the glory realm.

Into the Glory 5

How to Explain Water Baptism

When water baptism was explained to me it was described as *an outward expression of an inward change.* I don't disagree with this statement, but I believe it is incomplete. After witnessing the work of God released at this important time in our life, I have a more in depth definition of what is happening spiritually in our hearts, minds and even our physical bodies.

The recent glory being released in baptism is demonstrating the spiritual truths of what Jesus accomplished for us and how it is actually experienced now in our lives. There are some things in the Bible that we believe exist for us later in the future. Now, in this season of glory being released in the Church, we are witnessing the manifestation of the biblical promises connected to water baptism in a way that I have not seen before.

I have a greater expectation for God to move in the lives of those being baptized than I used to. I believe that in this season of glory God is actually moving us into a realm that looks more like it did when the early Church baptized the new converts. What we are experiencing now with baptism, or *glory baptisms,* is a restoration to the Church of power encounters with the Holy Spirit which God has intended for water baptism all along. It is something that the Church accessed in the early years when the kingdom was expanding at an exponential rate. We are now entering into this realm again in the last days as the great harvest of souls is upon us.

With this thought in mind I have a much more in depth biblical definition of what water baptism really means. The following definition is based upon scriptures I will unfold later on in this book.

Baptism into Christ is the time that Father releases His blessing into our lives. This blessing heals us. It frees our minds and removes all the curses from generational ties and soul ties which wrap around our hearts.

The power of this blessing gives us a true identity as sons and daughters of the Most High God. It is in the moment of baptism that God can remove false identities spoken over us or experienced throughout the years of our life.

All the lies and accusations which have bound us to living a life below our destiny can be supernaturally removed by the invisible hand of God. It is a time of healing deliverance and freedom from all the chains which have kept us bound. It is in this time while in the water that God can heal our minds, our souls and our bodies.

Finally it is an intense encounter with God as our heavenly Father. In baptism we are immersed into a place in Christ where we can know and experience God the way Jesus knew Him as the Father. It is a time where His love is experienced in a way that many on earth have never known. It is a place where we meet "Abba Father, our Daddy God."

Can I say it in a little shorter way?
Baptism is where heavenly Father releases his blessing and love, which imparts identity and removes all the curses from our hearts.

I understand a new person coming into faith may not have a full theological understanding of water baptism. This is where the one who baptizes can help immensely by giving people a better sense of expectation of what is about to happen.

Even reading about this theological process is very helpful as a person begins to develop a mental framework for all that God has been doing in their life since being baptized. We don't need to know everything before we get baptized, but it is great to understand scripturally what has happened.

One of the thoughts presented to us in the New Testament to study is the practice that people were baptized immediately after expressing their faith in Jesus Christ. I wanted to know why this was so important to the early Church. What are the theological aspects of being baptized? Is baptism simply something we do because we are embracing our faith in Jesus Christ? Or is it something that allows us to have a spiritual experience?

The modern era of Christianity we are living in today continues this process in some extent. There are truly churches which lead people to Christ and have them follow in believer's baptism as soon as possible. Are they really expecting a release of glory?

There are other practices of baptism in our modern era of Christianity that are not quite following the biblical model of the New Testament. In some instances, there does not seem to be the same emphasis upon baptism. Some current practices of baptism include infant baptism, confirmation after educational classes, being baptized by the denominational church one is joining, and some people might be encouraged to be baptized for some other reason rather than they have had a profound encounter with Christ.

All of these might have sincere motives and reasons why they follow certain practices. But they are not experiencing the true glorious life changing power that is offered to us in the scriptures. On a personal level, I do not try to convince someone to get re-baptized. If a person tells me they have been baptized in the past, I don't ask a lot of questions to see if they meet my expectations.

Here I am providing a biblical explanation of what can happen when we are baptized into Jesus. I do not see a scriptural reason to stop a person from being baptized again if they so desire. I believe that God wants us to encounter His love and power through baptism by having a better biblical understanding of what can transpire. I also believe that we can experience this without being re-baptized. I believe our faith level is truly rising for these encounters in baptism as we continue to see it happening to others right before our eyes.

In the following pages, I will expound more upon the question of being baptized more than once.

Is Getting Baptized More Than Once Scripturally Wrong?

With these references we see that the Bible describes multiple applications to be applied with the concept of baptism. How do we correlate the biblical instruction that there is one baptism with these multiple references to baptisms?

> **Ephesians 4:3-6 (NLT)**
> [3] Make every effort to keep yourselves united in the Spirit, binding yourselves together with peace. [4] For there is one body and one Spirit, just as you have been called to one glorious hope for the future. [5] There is one Lord, one faith, one baptism, [6] and one God and Father, who is over all and in all and living through all.

I share this scripture regarding one baptism in the context of verses three through six to help us gain clarity. The Apostle Paul is referencing the importance of unity in the Body of Christ. Here God reveals to us that when we are baptized into Christ we are all united into one Lord, one faith, one baptism. We did not get baptized into different churches of Christ. We are all immersed into the same Body of Christ, and we should respect and protect this unity.

I was saved at First Baptist Church, baptized there, married there and licensed from there. After being licensed into the gospel ministry, I have served at Skyway Baptist Church, now Skyway Church. I did not grow up in a church or denominational setting and was saved at age nineteen. Once I was in ministry I found out that from a denominational perspective people coming into the Baptist Church would be re-baptized unless they had a "letter" stating they were baptized at a different Baptist Church.

That position never sat well with me from a theological perspective. I can understand from a practical viewpoint that it solved a lot of technical problems for people who always attend the Baptist Church. Skyway was different. We were seeing people come from many different denominational backgrounds which did not want to be baptized as a Baptist. I agreed with them; I was baptized as a Christian. We changed our position to agree with the scriptural view that there is *one baptism.*

This biblical thought that there is one baptism is not contradicting the biblical instructions regarding the doctrine of baptisms. We are all baptized one time into Christ and his body. The powerful applications of baptism found in scripture are many. From my study of the scriptures being baptized in water more than one time is not violating our faith. The Spirit of God is speaking to the believer to make a new profession and acceptance of what God is doing in them for this time that is different than what happened many years before.

From what we are seeing and experiencing with people who have previously been baptized, being re-baptized is different. There is one baptism into Christ, but there are different biblical aspects of what happens at baptism. If a person chooses to express faith towards God through the act of baptism they are not sinning against God or making light of their faith. It is an act of faith on their part with which we are cooperating. The results of the work of the Spirit show us that these acts of faith are acceptable by God as he sends Holy Spirit to move in their lives.

In conclusion, this passage declaring one baptism does not negate or contradict the other New Testament baptisms discussed. The following is a testimony from a former pastor.

> *I had been baptized in water before but there was obviously something special happening for people as they were being "baptized into Glory". Having pastored previously and been a student of the Bible, I saw this encounter as something new and special that God was doing. In my opinion there was no theological conflict, so my wife and I decided to be baptized as a rededication of our marriage vows with God. As soon as I stepped into the water, it was obvious to me that God's presence was there. I could barely stand … it was like I was in a different dimension. I could see Jesus watching me through a veil with a look of complete acceptance and love. For a time I could not stand even though I was trying. After a while, my body began twisting as if I was being spun like a top. I pictured chains being pulled off as I twisted in the water. It was quite an experience with God and my wife, and we have entered into a greater dimension of love for each other. We didn't think it could get any better, but our relationship together has ascended to a greater level. We also sense a greater ability to minister to others. The gifts of the Spirit flow easier whenever we pray, especially the prophetic, and our teaching/preaching gifts seem more enhanced.*

We are excited to watch God move through us, and we are convinced the baptism experience was a breakthrough for us as we pursue God's destiny for us.

Fred Paine

Into the Glory

6

Baptism from a Hebrew Point of View

Before discussing this topic, I want to ensure you that I am not trying to take people and put them under the yoke of the Law. Much is written in order to stop us from becoming legalistic or ritualistic. Jesus came so that we can be free from trying to keep the Mosaic Law. It is impossible for anyone to successfully abide by the Law of Moses. If we could, Jesus would never have needed to die on the cross for our sins to be forgiven.

> **Galatians 3:11-13(NASB)**
> [11] Now that no one is justified by the Law before God is evident; for, "THE RIGHTEOUS MAN SHALL LIVE BY FAITH." [12] However, the Law is not of faith; on the contrary, "HE WHO PRACTICES THEM SHALL LIVE BY THEM." [13] Christ redeemed us from the curse of the Law, having become a curse for us—for it is written, "CURSED IS EVERYONE WHO HANGS ON A TREE"—

Once we have entered into our relationship with God through faith, we must guard our relationship and be careful that we are not going back by somehow trusting in our works to try and please God. So with this in mind, what use is it to read the Levitical Law as a Christian today? What can we learn about God's work in baptism today by what happened before Jesus came?

Today we can learn the *principles and the ways of God* by reading the Old Testament. We will never again be required to offer a blood sacrifice or perform any ritual listed in these writings. But we can read them and stop and ask the Holy Spirit to reveal to us the heart of God behind the rituals He required Israel to perform. This is why we are studying baptism from a Hebrew point of view.

Why did the priest and people have so many *mikvehs or washings?* As I have read through the many scriptures giving the circumstances connected to the acts of ritual washings, I see that they all are connected to major moments in a person's life. Some moments were like dealing with the trauma of finding a dead body. Another was the trauma of dealing with terrible sickness and illness. Others were when a priest would prepare for his ministry to serve the people. Finally, the important act of marriage required washings.

Let's think about these for a moment. In order to keep the Law, a person was required to stop what they were doing and spend a significant amount of time going through a process. This process was to give them access to God's help in order to get beyond something painful or move into something new and challenging. That, in and of itself, is worth noting.

In today's world, life is pretty much the same for the people of faith and those who choose to not live in faith. We go through life at a rapid pace. We encounter various trials, traumas and events of high stress both positive and negative. We do this without slowing down to emotionally acknowledge what we are going through. We push through, press on and man up.

Today there is no Law requiring us to stop what we are doing and go through a process that requires time out from our busy schedule. There are no priests who say we must go remove our clothes, bathe and then destroy the garments of the trauma, be inspected and then be sent back into service.

The closest thing we have to something like this process is found in the business world. Certain jobs require an employee who has encountered great stress on the job to see a therapist and be certified to return to their position. There is a reason these high stress jobs make this requirement. It is because in order to function properly the person needs to be whole. Even in these types of jobs people tend to feel bound up by these requirements; they want to push on with adrenaline, will power and emotional masking.

As I read these Levitical requirements, I can see the mercy of God. Something happens to our soul when we are touched by death. Something is going to be required of our heart and emotions as we embark into marriage or ministry. The washings requirements were a place where a person had to stop their activity. They had to focus on the matter at hand and ask God to help them through that season of life.

Another example of this today is when a person realizes that the stressors they are facing are too great for them to handle alone. They ask for someone to give them counsel and/or prayer. They stop adding more stress to their life until they deal with the mountains of inner stress and pain that have built up over time.

This same mercy is being released in the Glory Baptisms at this time. Going back to my opening statement, *glory is God's solution to gross darkness.* I am seeing the stress and trauma many people have carried in their souls being removed while they spend ten to fifteen minutes uninterrupted with God in the baptismal water. I see the fluttering eyelids which show me they are gone to a place with our merciful Father to have their souls washed and restored. People are taking time from their busy schedules. Many are buying airline tickets to come and let God wash away things they did not even know were affecting them until it was gone.

I believe in and practice Bible based counseling. I believe in and practice deliverance ministry. In each of these cases I must say that God can do more in the life of a person during the time they are in the Glory Baptism waters than in many hours with me in counseling or deliverance. The glory is the difference. It is releasing people in a way that person to person ministry cannot do. This is an amazing aspect of what God is doing in the baptismal waters.

I ask for you to keep this in mind as we look at the Hebrew perspective of baptism. These washings were instrumental in keeping God's people emotionally and physically fit for service. As we are preparing to be *Glory Carriers* to a world engulfed in gross darkness, we must first prepare ourselves for this task. It appears that one key way for this to happen is through the Glory Baptisms.

Hebrews Believers Had a Doctrine of Baptism (s)

> **Hebrews 6:2 (NLT)**
> ² You don't need further instruction about baptisms…

The writer to the Hebrews concludes that the audience did not need further instructions about the doctrine of baptisms. This one statement given to the particular audience, *Hebrew believers*, reveals that Hebrews who were familiar with the scriptures which Jesus read had further insights about baptisms or washings.

The Old Testament foreshadowed all that is available to us through Christ. This allows us to fully appreciate all that we have access to as his followers. As we read it, we understand the fullness of what God is making available to us now that we are in Christ Jesus. In these passages we will learn in our modern day world what the Hebrew Christians knew when the book of Hebrews was written.

The Greek word for baptism is Baptizo, and the Hebrew word is Mikveh. Each of these words is translated *to immerse*. Now, the scriptures might have a different word other than immerse, but the concept being described is essentially the same. Both words mean to be immersed into another substance and being saturated. We are immersed and saturated into Christ, the Body or Church, The Holy Spirit, the cleansing Fire of God and personal sozo - healing and deliverance.

Let's take a moment and connect the rituals of the Old Testament with the practice of believers under a new covenant. First and foremost, I must say that we do not need to go and be baptized every time a cleansing is needed in our life. The Bible teaches us that today in the New Covenant we have our conscience cleaned by the blood of Jesus and by the washing of the water of his word.

> **Hebrews 9:14 (KJV)**
> [14] How much more shall the blood of Christ, who through the eternal Spirit offered himself without spot to God, purge your conscience from dead works to serve the living God?
>
> **Ephesians 5:25-27 (KJV)**
> [25] ...Christ also loved the church, and gave himself for it;
> [26] That he might sanctify and cleanse it with the washing of water by the word,

This reference starts with the relationship between husbands and wives. Paul connects the Old Testament ritual of the bride washing before her marriage with Christ cleansing the church. In both of these passages, the follower of Christ gains understanding that much of what was done through the religious rites of baptism in the Old Covenant are now spiritually available to every believer, every single day, through our faith in Christ and the power of his word over us.

We should first come to God through prayer asking for His cleansing of our hearts, minds and souls. We can do this because Jesus shed his blood for us to be whole and clean. We can declare the promises of God's word to wash us and cleanse us from the contaminations of the world that cling to us. But what if after we do everything we know to do we still need more freedom?

Sometimes We Need to Wash our Feet, Other Times the Whole Body!

On the night before Jesus went to the cross, He took a towel and basin and began to wash the feet of his disciples. Peter was quick to object and say that Jesus would not serve him like a servant. Jesus told him that if he did not let Him wash him, he was not properly connected to Him. This led Peter to the conclusion that He wanted Jesus to give him a complete bath! Jesus brought Peter back into a perspective that still holds true to us today. We get dirty in this world and the part of us that gets dirty needs to be washed. Let's look at how Jesus spoke to Peter about washing his feet...

> **John 13:10 (NASB)**
> [10] Jesus said to him, "He who has bathed needs only to wash his feet, but is completely clean; and you are clean, but not all *of you*."

As we walk in this world we are coming in contact with things that cling to us. These things are like dirt on our feet that needs to be washed off. Praying and declaring God's word over ourselves and with others is usually all we need to be free of the darkness connected to those experiences in life. This is what we teach and practice on a regular basis.

There are other times where we have gone through some difficult experiences that seem to slow us down. These times in our life drain us of our faith, and we start going through the motions.

Have you ever had a computer that had a virus? It starts to run slower and slower. You know what your computer is supposed to do and has done in the past, but now it has something attached that is attacking it. Some viruses are easy to get rid of and others are not. These viruses can cause us to take our computer to a specialist to get them removed. Once the virus is taken out, the computer goes back to working like it did originally.

That is what I have been seeing in the Glory Baptisms. God, the specialist, is setting people free from all sorts of spiritual viruses which have vexed their lives. There are things people have been through over the years which have gotten into their souls like a virus. I mean things they have prayed about, confessed and have done everything they know to do. Some have gone to counseling. Others have gone through Christian deliverance. Still, like a virus, they are not living in the freedom they know that Christ provides.

Some others have experienced powerful deliverances which they were not even aware were affecting them until after their baptism experiences. In the end, the glory of God being released in this season is setting God's people free to be the glory carriers for the next move of God taking place.

Into the Glory 7

Baptism in the New Testament

When we start reading the New Testament, one of the first events discussed, as the ministry of Jesus is introduced and begins, is the concept of baptism. John the Baptist was sent as the forerunner of Christ. His ministry was to prepare people to embrace Jesus. He introduced Jesus as the Lamb of God who takes away the sins of the world. John was directed by God to baptize people who demonstrated their repentance of sins. They followed in baptism because of their willingness to be ready to enter into and experience a new season of the kingdom of God.

The fact that so many were ready to embrace John's message and method of baptism reflects that the origin of baptism was already understood and embraced before the writing of the New Testament.

As we read throughout the New Testament, eight different references to baptism are found. Hebrews chapter six gives reference to the doctrines of baptisms plural. This implies a foundational understanding about this doctrine of which Hebrew followers of Christ had already been clearly instructed. Next we see eight references in the New Testament to baptism experiences.

1. The baptism of John Ref. John 3:23
2. The baptism of Jesus Ref John 3:26
3. The baptism into Christ, His Body, His death Ephesians 4:5
4. The baptism of suffering Matthew 20:23
5. The baptism of the Holy Spirit Acts 1:8
6. The baptism of Fire Matthew 3:11
7. The baptism of Israel into Moses 1 Corinthians 10:1-4
8. The doctrine of baptisms Hebrews 6:2

The New Testament History of Immediate Baptism

One of my thoughts when reading the Bible was *why did they get baptized immediately?* This question was instrumental in my study and gaining insights that I will share regarding what really takes place when a person is baptized.

I am not of a theological belief that a person must be baptized to be saved. I am aware that some view certain scriptures to promote this belief. I believe our eternal salvation is based completely upon one's personal expression of faith in Christ's forgiveness of sins. We must trust His death on the cross and resurrection of life to be all sufficient for eternal salvation. Salvation is a personal experience we enter into because our hearts and minds are opened to see Jesus as the Son of God, the Savior of the world.

Yet in Peter's first sermon, baptism is an essential element that is not something we should take lightly nor do at a random time later. They took the time to baptize three thousand people that very day! Why? What did they know about baptism that is so important for people to embrace it immediately?

The next time we see immediate baptism described is in Acts chapter eight. Again we see that this government official had the desire to be saved and also follow in immediate baptism. This could not have been a small event with the government entourage traveling with him. It was something that could not be delayed.

Acts chapter eight introduces us to Saul of Tarsus who will be known later as the Apostle Paul. He was filled with rage persecuting the Church when he had his supernatural encounter with Christ on the Damascus road. A key believer at that time, Ananias, was sent to bring Saul completely into the Way of Christ which included getting baptized immediately and experiencing the infilling of the Holy Spirit.

> **Acts 9:17-18 (NASB)**
> [17] So Ananias departed and entered the house, and after laying his hands on him said, "Brother Saul, the Lord Jesus, who appeared to you on the road by which you were coming, has sent me so that you may regain your sight and be filled with the Holy Spirit." [18] And immediately there fell from his eyes something like scales, and he regained his sight, and he got up and was baptized;

The pattern continues again in Acts chapter ten with the conversion of Cornelius and his group. This was the first time the Church included Gentiles or those who were not Jewish, as believers. This would continue to be a pressing issue throughout the writings of the New Testament. It is important for us to see this key moment of salvation continued to include water baptism and experiencing demonstrations of the Holy Spirit in their lives. This is similar to the other biblical accounts of what was transpiring as the early Church was growing and expanding the Kingdom of God throughout the known world.

Next, we see the Gospel expanding into Europe in Acts chapter sixteen with the conversion of Lydia and her entire family. The connection between salvation, immediate baptism and the power of the Spirit continues.

This would lead to Paul and Silas preaching the gospel with signs and wonders resulting in their imprisonment. God miraculously sets them free resulting in the salvation of the man in charge of the prison.

> **Acts 16:27-33 (NASB)**
> 27 When the jailer awoke and saw the prison doors opened, he drew his sword and was about to kill himself, supposing that the prisoners had escaped. 28 But Paul cried out with a loud voice, saying, "Do not harm yourself, for we are all here!" 29 And he called for lights and rushed in, and trembling with fear he fell down before Paul and Silas, 30 and after he brought them out, he said, "Sirs, what must I do to be saved?" 31 They said, "Believe in the Lord Jesus, and you will be saved, you and your household." 32 And they spoke the word of the Lord to him together with all who were in his house. 33 And he took them that *very* hour of the night and washed their wounds, and immediately he was baptized, he and all his *household.*

I have taken the time to share all of these New Testament passages to demonstrate that the biblical history of the Church is filled with people following the Lord in water baptism immediately after conversion. In these recorded accounts it is normal to see supernatural manifestations and lives completely transformed as all of this transpires.

This same glorious power continues to be released to us today as we are baptizing. The glory of God showed up the first night and is still miraculously strong every time we baptize even as I am writing this book. People are arriving early with hunger and expectation for God to move. This is all a part of how the glory is being released. *People were baptized immediately because God uses baptism to change our lives!*

Jesus Commands All to Be Baptized

As we have read, we can see that there is so much God wants to do in our lives and baptism is an essential part of it. For some, the Glory Baptism, might be a new time spent with Father in the water. Others who are being baptized for the first time are now having the same types of experiences with God. We are seeing everyone who is baptized experiencing God's glory and power. Watching what God is doing helps us to understand why Jesus commanded us to go into all the nations and baptize the disciples. Baptism is a crucial element of our spiritual breakthrough.

> **Matthew 28:19-20 (NASB)** [19] "Go therefore and make disciples of all the nations, baptizing them in the name of the Father and the Son and the Holy Spirit, [20] teaching them to observe all that I commanded you; and lo, I am with you always, even to the end of the age."

What if this experience we are having right now with all these people who are being baptized became the norm for all the future people yet to be baptized? What if it was normal for healings, miracles and restorations of the hearts and minds to happen all over the world when people were baptized?

Think about the radical shifts taking place in all spheres of society if people had these kinds of encounters as a regular daily experience around the world. It would certainly make it easier to teach the nations about God if tens of thousands and hundreds of thousands and even millions of people are having life changing encounters when they get baptized. This is a shift the Church desperately needs as we move forward into world evangelism. The glory of God being released in these baptism experiences is a return to the glory that God released in the beginning.

The Baptism of John

When John the Baptist came baptizing, people were ready to receive his message and follow his method of baptism which he promoted. Why did people come from all over Israel to follow John and be baptized into repentance?

The reason it was accepted was because baptism was already a part of the Hebrew culture. Our Christian baptism came from these very roots. The reason I am sharing this information is because the fruit of what we are seeing take place aligns with what the Hebrews believed and experienced in baptism long ago.

Everything in the Old Testament was a picture of the fullness which we can experience in Jesus Christ. What people experienced in part before Christ we can now experience in complete fullness. We now know the source of God's life and power is available to us through Jesus, the Son of God.

Let's look at some New Testament Scriptures that show us that Jesus, the Apostles and early Church knew more about baptism from their background in worshiping God.

> **John 3:23-25 (NASB)**
> [23] John also was baptizing in Aenon near Salim, because there was much water there; and *people* were coming and were being baptized— [24] for John had not yet been thrown into prison. [25] Therefore there arose a discussion on the part of John's disciples with a Jew about purification.

Notice that verse twenty five states there was a discussion about *purification* which also translates baptism. They knew there were different baptisms connected to helping people become cleansed or healed from the emotional trauma they experienced in life.

The general thought presented by God to His people was that going through water purification, or baptism, gave them a new cleansing and healing from the past season. It would allow them to be free to move forward into their next season.

Look at these notes from the Bible Background Commentary on the scripture from John 3:25-26...

> On Jewish ceremonial purification, cf. John 2:6 and John 11:55. This theme runs through the Gospel: ceremonial washing (John 2:6), proselyte baptism (John 3:5), perhaps Jacob's well (John 4) and the healing waters of Bethesda (John 5), Siloam's water for the Feast of Tabernacles (John 7:37-38; John 9:7) and perhaps John 13:5-11 and John 19:34.
>
> *(Bible Background Commentary - The IVP BibleBackground Commentary – New Testament.)*

All of these locations were connected with water. Water is essential in God's plan for creating, restoring and cleansing.

> **1 Peter 3:21 (NASB)**
> [21] Corresponding to that, baptism now saves you—not the removal of dirt from the flesh, but an appeal to God for a good conscience—through the resurrection of Jesus Christ,

This scripture does not promote the belief that one must be baptized to experience eternal life as some propose. It is stating that God has chosen baptism as the method of releasing His *Sozo* into our life. *Sozo* refers to healing of the realm of the conscience where our thoughts, memories and experiences of life can affect our physical body and daily well-being.

Here is the definition of this word...

> *sōzō*
>
> *"to save," is sometimes used of "healing" or "restoration to health," the latter in John 11:12, RV, "he will recover," marg., "be saved" (AV, "he shall do well"). See HEAL, PRESERVE, SAVE, WHOLE.*

(Vine's Expository Dictionary of Old Testament and New Testament Words.)

This verse of scripture is stating that God has chosen baptism for us to experience healing and restoration resulting in health and recovery.

Into the Glory 8

The Baptism of Jesus

Matthew 3:13-15 (NASB)

¹³ Then Jesus *arrived from Galilee at the Jordan *coming* to John, to be baptized by him. ¹⁴ But John tried to prevent Him, saying, "I have need to be baptized by You, and do You come to me?" ¹⁵ But Jesus answering said to him, "Permit *it* at this time; for in this way it is fitting for us to fulfill all righteousness." Then he *permitted Him.

We know that John the Baptist baptized people into the *baptism of repentance*. He did not want to baptize Jesus because Jesus did not have sin. He did not need to repent. This is why John could not figure out why Jesus had come for baptism. The answer which Jesus gave to John is a clue for all of us about the significance of our water baptism experience. He said it was fitting to fulfill all *righteousness*.

The whole doctrine of the righteousness of God is very important. You can go to school for years and learn more and more about this. I am glad that God does not make us go to school before He allows us to experience what it truly means. The Greek word used here is *dikaiosynē*. The simplest definition for this word is, *to be in right standing with God*. It can also mean to do the right thing.

In this passage Jesus tells us that He is fulfilling righteousness. Let me put it this way; when Jesus was baptized He became the *Pattern Son* for all the emerging believers who will be baptized in the future. When He was baptized He was providing a way for all of us to personally experience what it is like to be right with God. Righteousness is more than a theological doctrine; it is an inner peace that God in heaven accepts us. This acceptance of *being right* is something we can experience.

Let's next examine how this manifestation of righteousness was experienced by Jesus when he was baptized.

> **Matthew 3:16-17 (NASB)**
> [16] After being baptized, Jesus came up immediately from the water; and behold, the heavens were opened, and he saw the Spirit of God descending as a dove *and* lighting on Him, [17] and behold, a voice out of the heavens said, "This is My beloved Son, in whom I am well-pleased."

When Jesus came out of the water there was an audible voice that other people actually heard. God pronounced His approval and acceptance upon his Son. Jesus had never preached a sermon. He had not healed a person. He had not even started making any disciples. God pronounced His approval upon Jesus *because of their relationship.* God's approval was announced, "He is right with Me!"

Another way of looking at this baptism experience is that *Jesus received the blessing of Heavenly Father.* This blessing gave Jesus His *true identity*. This blessing gave Him the strength to stand up to the devil's accusations in the wilderness. He knew he was the Son of God. He had no problem when the devil or anyone else tried to question him about who He was or His relationship with Father.

The *Blessing of the Father* is a key part of the *wells of baptism* which are now opened. This is a scriptural key I have tapped into when I pray for people during the baptisms. When the person comes up out of the water I make a biblical decree that *you are truly God's accepted son or daughter. I now release the blessing of Father God upon you. I can say this over you because the Bible says God gave you the right to be called a child of God.* Your baptism is where *impartation of your right to be a child of God Most High* is released over your life.

> **John 1:12-13 (NASB)**
> ¹² But as many as received Him, to them He gave the right to become children of God, *even* to those who believe in His name, ¹³ who were born, not of blood nor of the will of the flesh nor of the will of man, but of God.

Every time I have released Father's blessing it has a profound effect upon the person. It is not unusual for people to shake or cry. I see those who have never had a blessing spoken over them feel a new inner acceptance for the very first time. It is very personal and amazing to be a part of this moment people have with God.

I do not personally know the background of most people so I simply pray what I feel God wants me to pray when I release this blessing. Many testimonies have come back to me saying, "It was your voice but I heard my Heavenly Father speaking to me." Others have said, "I don't know what you said, but I went somewhere with God and He gave me such peace." *I found that when I agree with what the scriptures say is possible we open a heavenly door over people to actually experience what it is like to be blessed by God.*

The second key I have accessed in opening the wells of baptism *is giving room for the Holy Spirit to move in the person's life while they are baptized.* There was a physical manifestation of the Holy Spirit at the baptism of Jesus. The scriptures read that the Holy Spirit came *as a dove.* This phrase reveals that the movement of the Spirit at baptism was evident to everyone involved.

I feel the component of giving people access to the true moving of the Holy Spirit is essential for each person being baptized. This allows them to really experience the fullness of the moment with God. Many New Testament scriptures about baptism include the Holy Spirit touching the lives of those being baptized like this...

> **Acts 10:46-47 (NASB)**
> 46 For they were hearing them speaking with tongues and exalting God. Then Peter answered,
> 47 "Surely no one can refuse the water for these to be baptized who have received the Holy Spirit just as we did, can he?"

In our Glory Baptism services I invite our ministers who have been moving in this new glory realm to join me at the services. Those who are going to be baptized are invited to allow these glory carriers to spend time praying for them. This is a special part of the baptism services. Of course these ministry teams also provide the same ministry for others who come out and are not being baptized.

There are many testimonies about the accuracy of what has been prayed by these ministers bringing great comfort and peace. These ministers also hear and share prophetic insights about God's purposes for their life. It is not unusual to hear that many different people shared the same thoughts through prayer with those who are being baptized as each different prayer team prayed over them.

All of this prepares people for coming into the baptismal waters. This is what I refer to as coming into the *Glory Zone*. It is amazing to watch how the Holy Spirit touches people when they walk down the steps into the water. I had one man, Randy, tell me that his feet stopped moving. The look on his face was priceless.

Randy is not someone who chases signs and wonders. He would be considered conservative by most people. He did not want to miss out on the fruit of what God was doing. If God was moving in a new way that could change his life for the better, he was open to experience it. He really did not expect to have the Holy Spirit move like this physically in the water the way he did. But even better, things at his business have drastically changed for the better. People from nearby businesses are dropping in on a regular basis, because they like being around Randy and Terri. They say that they can feel something different about them. People coming into the business are now asking for prayer. One customer even confided that they were dealing with cancer. After agreeing to let them pray, the customer later returned with the miracle report that the cancer was gone! Praise God! There is lasting fruit from these encounters in the glory.

The third key of the unlocking the wells of baptism is *the removal of curses*. Now, Jesus did not have any curses to have removed, but the rest of us surely do. Many will do the best they can to get by in life and suffer through a lot of emotional and spiritual baggage along the way. This was never God's plan for us. Look at what the scriptures say is available for us when we are baptized...

> **Colossians 2:8-15 (NASB)**
> 8 See to it that no one takes you captive through philosophy and empty deception, according to the tradition of men, according to the elementary principles of the world, rather than according to Christ. 9 For in Him all the fullness of Deity dwells in bodily form, 10 and in Him you have been made complete, and He is the head over all rule and authority; 11 and in Him you were also circumcised with a circumcision made without hands, in the removal of the body of the flesh by the circumcision of Christ; 12 having been buried with Him in baptism, in which you were also raised up with Him through faith in the working of God, who raised Him from the dead. 13 When you were dead in your transgressions and the

uncircumcision of your flesh, He made you alive together with Him, having forgiven us all our transgressions, ¹⁴ having canceled out the certificate of debt consisting of decrees against us, which was hostile to us; and He has taken it out of the way, having nailed it to the cross. ¹⁵ When He had disarmed the rulers and authorities, He made a public display of them, having triumphed over them through Him.

When we read all of these verses together we can grasp the magnitude of what can happen for us when we get baptized. *Verse twelve tells us that the key moment for experiencing these promises is during our baptism.* We *were buried with Him at baptism*. We need to get what is being expressed here to us. When someone dies everything against them ends. *Baptism is the END of every decree, debt and curse ever made against you.*

Looking at verses eight and nine together can change our lives. Verse eight warns us that there are principles in this world we live in that can deceive us and keep us hostage even if we are truly believers in Jesus Christ. It is biblically possible to be saved and still be taken captive. BUT...

In Jesus we are made complete. Remember the words about righteousness we just previously read? This is that. When we make Jesus the Lord of our life and ask him for forgiveness he says, "You are complete." The world and the devil will try to convince us that we need to do something religious to get *more saved.* In reality your faith filled your heavenly bank account with righteousness; YOU ARE COMPLETELY ALRIGHT with God.

Do you want to know what God is doing in our hearts when we get baptized? Verses ten and eleven tell us that Jesus is more powerful than any dark spirit that we have ever encountered in our past. He is more powerful than any group of spirits that may have been in our family tree. Before we are saved, we don't have the spiritual power to shake them out of our tree. We are trapped with them tormenting us and chaining up our hearts with curses and pain. All of that gets broken by Jesus the all-powerful One when we are baptized.

The Bible uses a play on words in verse eleven. Here we read that God *circumcises our hearts.* Circumcision was the sign of covenant in the Old Testament. All the males' young or old had to be circumcised as a sign or symbol of their relationship with God. Now in the New Testament, *baptism is the sign of covenant with God.*

Baptism is where the invisible hand of God cuts away all the things which have wounded us, hurt us and ensnared us. After I speak God's blessing over people in the baptismal water, I decree that God is removing every curse. Every generational curse, every soul tie and every chain is now being removed by the hand of God.

It is amazing what begins to happen with people when I do this. I see the chains of rejections coming off their heart. I see the arrows of evil words spoken removed. Hurtful words and abandonment are removed. It is as if in that moment with Daddy God, every snare ever designed to keep us bound is being evicted and cut away by the hand of God.

I remember speaking with one man who was set free by the hand of God. In previous encounters with him it would appear that he was trying so hard in every area of his life. Trying hard to be spiritual, to be liked, to be accepted and approved. He was a good guy, but he was trapped in his search for the approval of others. After his glory baptism experience with Daddy God, he was at peace. Our conversation did not have that tension. He was at peace and it allowed me to be at peace visiting with him. God had blessed him with acceptance and removed all the striving for approval all at one time.

Dani was another person who had something very powerful removed from her heart during her glory baptism. As a deliverance minister, she is very careful to walk pure and keep herself spiritually clean. She has gone through many sessions of renunciation to break curses and ties off her life. She would be one that most would think all the old stuff is broken off.

I remember during her baptism that I broke a *regional curse* off of her heart. When I said this, she began to shake violently and became all red in the skin. Suddenly it all left. Later she explained to me that she had never thought about the overarching spirit in the region of Bulgaria where she grew up. It was filled with poverty, jealousy and darkness. Somehow, in that moment in the water God declared that those soul ties to her geographic home were broken. She was glowing with glory as she told me how free she felt after this was removed from her heart.

Now Dani has been going to other states and even into Mexico baptizing people and seeing them set free in glory baptisms. This deliverance from God is available to everyone who is *In Christ*. This is a biblical truth that gives me faith for everyone I see to be free from chains and bondages. *I have great faith for deliverance to be quick and not embarrassing.*

Look at this wonderful promise to us regarding baptism...

> **Romans 6:3-4 (NASB)**
> ³ Or do you not know that all of us who have been baptized into Christ Jesus have been baptized into His death?
> ⁴ Therefore we have been buried with Him through baptism into death, so that as Christ was raised from the dead through the glory of the Father, so we too might walk in newness of life.

As I have stated earlier, *Baptizo,* literally means *to immerse*. It means more than simply dipping something into water. It has the connotation to mean that whatever is *baptized takes on the properties of what it is baptized into.* If you took white cloth and baptized it into purple dye, you would never call the cloth white any longer. It would now be called purple cloth because the baptism of the white cloth into the purple dye.

We are no longer the same old person after we are baptized into Christ. We are literally empowered by the Spirit of God to become new. We are empowered or changed to walk in a new way of life! This transformation is made available through our baptism.

God wants us all to access this glory at any stage of our walk with Him. I was ministering at Glory of Zion in Corinth, Texas, about this subject. There was no water, no baptisms and I did not personally touch anyone while I prayed. This story came from a man named Chris who came up to me after the service ended.

Chris said that while I was praying for the glory to be released at the end of the service, he fell over in the Spirit. His spirit was lifted up and he could look down at his body lying on the chairs. He then encountered Jesus. Jesus asked Chris to walk with Him so they started walking up the aisle of the church together. As they walked, Jesus said, "Chris, there is some darkness inside you I need to take out."

Suddenly Chris saw his own chest cavity opened with his organs inside with dark black spots all around. He thought Jesus was going to take out the physical organs. Next, Jesus was holding something that looked like a jar of glory. He took the shining glory from the jar and placed it inside of Chris' chest cavity. Suddenly all the darkness was gone and Jesus closed him up. They walked together back towards where his body was still lying on the chairs. Jesus said, "It is time to go back." Chris told me how wonderful it was walking with Jesus and he said, "I want to stay here with you." Jesus replied to him, "No, you need to go back and give what I gave to you away to others." Suddenly Chris shot back into his body and he came to as if waking up.

I am convinced that the new move of God's glory is preparing all of us to be free of the things that have hurt us and kept us bound. Many have not yet recognized what some of these things are that are living in them. God does not want to embarrass us or condemn us. He wants to heal us, fill us with glory and then send us out to give this glory to others. It can happen in the baptism waters or it can happen while lying on a chair. The most important part is to believe it can happen and put ourselves in a position for God to move in our lives.

Baptism prepares us for Public Ministry

One of the doctrines of baptisms in the Old Testament dealt with preparing a priest for public ministry. Jesus was baptized before He began his public ministry. He was following this concept of personal preparation and sanctification before the Father.

There is something similar taking place with the Glory Baptisms. The amount of leaders coming to be baptized is astounding. One of the literal definitions of the word glory is weighty. There is a tangible, significant weighty glory being released when I am baptizing leaders.

It is normal for people to be "slain in the Spirit" or float in a state of being out in the water. As I hold them I am aware of when a manifestation of the Spirit takes place which I call a *glory wave*. These heavy, weighty waves physically push the person back or down in the water.

This happens to most everyone but it seems to have a stronger demonstration of glory when leaders are being baptized. The same is true when healing and deliverance occurs. The strong call of leadership on the life of the person seems to multiply the power of the glory being released in the water.

The testimonies of the leaders coming back to me are consistent with the experiences of increased spiritual discernment. They are also experiencing greater anointing power for signs and wonders and greater clarity for prophetic words and words of knowledge.

Into the Glory

Here is a testimony of one of the leaders who has been baptized into the Glory.

The night I went through the Glory Baptism changed my life forever. As I stepped into the water that October night, I knew something was going to happen. Pastor Greg baptized my wife first and just before my wife went under the water, I saw an Angel fly down into the water. When my wife came back up out of the water, she was so radiant and glowing! It was so beautiful and then it was my turn. I went under the water and I knew he brought me back up, but I wasn't there; I had left and gone to heaven! You see, a number of years ago I died and went to Heaven. At that time I was greeted by an Angel of the Lord. I was shown things around Heaven and things about the future of the earth and then sent back. That same Angel greeted me again. He showed me and told me things about the future of the earth... but I also got to see Jesus and hug Him as well!

After my Glory Baptism, I have been preaching in different places in the USA and South Korea. I released the Glory to the people of South Korea. Some started to cry while others were rocking back and forth, and some couldn't even hold their heads up anymore as the heavy Glory fell on them! This didn't happen just once, but every service I was in after that! I am a Glory Carrier and wherever I go, I bring the Glory with me, and I release it on everyone. I have been set on FIRE now, way beyond anything I have ever experienced!

Ivan Tuttle

Into the Glory

The Knowledge of the Glory

Habakkuk 2:14 (NASB)
14 "For the earth will be filled With the knowledge of the glory of the LORD, As the waters cover the sea.

When I first heard about God pouring out his glory on our state I wondered what it would look like. How can this happen, and how will we recognize it? My concern is that a concept like the *glory of the Lord* will remain an abstract, subjective experience. We can *feel the glory* but what does that really mean? Is the glory something more than a goose bump or joyful expression? Is it more than excited Pentecostalism?

When I heard about the glory covering Arizona and springing forth into a global awakening I began studying many verses of scripture regarding the glory. I wanted to know if there were tangible expressions and experiences regarding God's glory that we could actually recognize and monitor.

Here in Habakkuk we see that God promises there will be a day when the *knowledge of the glory* will fill the earth. He did not simply say the glory would fill the earth. If this were the case, every sunset, majestic mountain and powerful wave from the ocean would fill the earth with the glory of God. But God says that *the knowledge of the glory* will fill the earth. This means that the earth will experience God's glory in such a way that it can be recognized and appreciated by everyone on a global scale.

The word *knowledge* is the Hebrew word Yada. Here is the first biblical definition I was able to study.

> *Knowledge*
> *Essentially yāda' means: (1) to know by observing and reflecting (thinking), and (2) to know by experiencing. The first sense appears in Gen. 8:11 where Noah "knew" the waters had abated as a result of seeing the freshly picked olive leaf in the dove's mouth; he "knew" it after observing and thinking about what he had seen. He did not actually see or experience the abatement himself.*

Vine's Expository Dictionary of Old Testament and New Testament Words.

There is a powerful insight regarding the first time a word is used in scripture. I call this the principle of the first. In this principle we see a word revealed that will continue to be unveiled each time it is used throughout the remainder of the scriptures. In this regard, Yada shows us that Noah observed and reflected on that which was brought into his realm of awareness. His knowledge started him on a journey of awareness to come to a conclusion. This is an important concept for us to gain as we discuss the glory of God in the emerging season. With this definition in place, we can say that God is going to reveal aspects of Himself to the entire world in a way that will cause people everywhere to seek to know and understand him better.

Yada is a versatile word and has several meanings depending on the context. Let's take a look at a few examples.

Yada is to know something or someone in complete detail. It means to study, analyze, or investigate something until you know something or someone completely. In this sense, we can say that the knowledge of the glory would be described as something we can analyze and investigate. The glory is going to have many distinct dimensions which people will be drawn to embrace.

This means that there will be a time when the entire earth is covered with people seeking to know more intimately and clearly what God is really all about. There will be a time when God is revealing His glory to people on the earth, and they in turn will be searching Him out. They will be coming from all aspects of life, not only Judeo-Christian backgrounds.

I am thinking about the *Magi* during the time of the birth of Jesus. They were actually men who studied the stars and realized from the phenomenon in the heavens that there was something or someone they had to investigate. This knowledge of the glory for them was a sign that was understandable in their world. This demonstration of glory caused them to enter into a journey to find the Christ. The glory changed their lives. God used them to warn Joseph of the coming persecution. These non-Jewish kings from afar changed history, because they investigated the glory.

The glory season is when the Lord is revealing Himself to those who desire to know Him. It is a time that spiritual people are seeking to know God. We must represent God to the world as one who cares about our aloneness not only our sinfulness.

The glory season is not a time to be judgmental of others' current behaviors or practices. God is using the glory to bring people to Him. Repentance is the work of the Spirit. We must be careful in this season to not pre-judge those who are attracted to the glory. They may be currently in other forms of religion. They may look different in their appearance. Their language for what God is doing may be different than those who have been Christians for years studying the Bible.

The glory will bring people from all aspects of life. Glory Carriers must be so filled with the love of the Father that they are not put off by the outward appearance of those who are seeking. This is why it is so important for the Glory Carriers to be baptized into the love and forgiveness of God. We must first be healed in our hearts to carry the true message of the glory to those who are seeking God in this season.

Yada: To technically know how something works

Another definition or dimension of yada is to know something technically. The owner of a watch knows what time it is. This is one type of knowledge, but the maker of the watch, yada or knows how the watch works to tell us the correct time. This is another realm of knowledge.

The technical aspects of getting something correct are fundamental in being able to repeat a process correctly over and over again. *The knowledge of the glory is going to be a season when we know how God is working*. He will let us in on His plans for mankind. We will understand how things work and be able to do them more than one miraculous time. We will never be able to create a *formula for God, but we will know what the Father is doing and partner with Him at the right place and right time.*

The third dimension of yada is to know God by personal experience. A lot of people know about God, but God wants us to know Him through encounters in which we personally experience His presence. The new move in the water baptism is one very real way people are having personal encounters with God the Father. I tell people every time before the baptisms start, "Don't expect the encounter someone else has had. Expect your own encounter because Father God knows exactly what you need in this moment." The many distinct and different testimonies coming forward in this hour all have the same common denominator: People are having personal encounters with God. These are encounters of love, freedom, healing and restoration. This is the time to see and experience God in this new light.

The fourth dimension of *yada* is to have a face-to-face encounter. It is much like the personal encounter just described. It takes us deeper into our encounter with Father. It is one thing to encounter God's goodness expressed in physical healing, forgiveness, intervention, provision, or blessing. It is entirely a different thing to have a face to face experience with Father. Even in some of these radical personal encounters, we fail to have a face to face with God.

God desires an up-close and personal face-to-face encounter. He does not desire an absentee relationship with His children. He wants to do more than send the things we need and desire from afar. No, His desire is to reveal himself to His children every day. Some children know that their dad will provide good things for them. Other children know the joy of knowing their good dad.

Face to face encounters can happen daily in our hearts. They are when our heart fills into our throats, and we get tears in our eyes. We feel an inner peace and security that is stronger than the fear trying to get into our hearts. God is revealing himself as a good Father in these encounters going on all around us.

The final dimension of *yada* is sexual intimacy, which causes us to reproduce. This is the realm of intimate knowledge of Father leading us to being fruitful in our lives.

Genesis 4:1 (KJV)
¹ And Adam knew Eve his wife; and she conceived, and bare Cain, and said, I have gotten a man from the LORD.

The scriptures teach us that Adam knew his wife, and she conceived. This was essential to fulfill the very first command God gave to man. God said we must be fruitful and multiple.

So many people are desperate to be fruitful in their lives. This is our greatest joy. In all my many years of Christian leadership I would say this is the greatest cry of the heart people have demonstrated. They are willing to go to classes and conferences. They will travel the world and serve their fellow man. All of this is in their sincere desire to be fruitful with their lives.

Many of the leaders in our ASCEND International Network have embraced being baptized into the glory. This has resulted in many examples of new dimension of fruitfulness in our lives and ministries. The number of doors that have opened after being baptized is astounding. Ministry opportunities to all seven mountains of culture have all been connected to the glory.

I recently met with our commissioned leaders, and we started giving testimonies of all the doors of ministry that have opened since we embraced the glory. There have been more miracles and healings reported in six months than I can remember in a lifetime. The number of souls being saved are increasing and lives are being changed by our ministries. The fruitfulness of the knowledge of the glory is amazing.

One such example is in a local city which has been marked by division. One of our leaders has served to unite over twenty churches, the government and businesses to bring revival to their city. The man who is leading this said that things took a tremendous turn for the fulfillment of this outreach once the glory carriers shifted the spirit realm with prayer.

Another one of our leaders had just invited our ASCEND International ministers to conduct a Glory River Explosion in her city. She is the president of the ministerial association. All the churches in the city were united for the glory to be released. Three months later we learned that the local government honored her with a key to the city. This is tangible evidence of the fruit multiplying in the glory!

There are many more examples of how the glory has changed the ministers, their ministries and the fruit of their labor. One of our governmental apostles led a key prayer team during the recent elections in Israel. Newspapers reported that Prime Minister Benjamin Netanyahu was trailing greatly in all the polls. After this key prayer journey was completed he made a *great come from behind victory!*

Others in our network are now taking the glory to other regions of our nation and to other nations. Rural areas of Indiana, Montana, Northern California, Colorado, and even into Mexico are all among the areas which have taken up the practice of Glory Baptisms and are reporting miracles. Our apostles in Juarez, Mexico have reported people are coming from surrounding cities into Juarez to be baptized in the glory. Since this has happened one of the largest drug lords in Mexico was recently captured in Juarez. God is shifting the atmosphere in the city known as the murder capital of the world by the glory!

Once people are filled with the glory the most important thing they can do is to give it away. This is what people are doing, and it is causing many more to move into the glory realm. I am amazed at the incredible amount of fruit that has unfolded in our network since we embraced the glory. If you are hungry to be fruitful in your life and ministry, now is the time to embrace the knowledge of glory fully.

Into the Glory 10

Word Studies about the Glory

One of the ways I have always looked at a subject is to do a biblical study of the words used. In this I look at the context of how a word is used and how do the various times it is used in scripture all connect. I look at biblical definitions and regular definitions. In this method I try to get a big picture of a topic while looking at how all the parts fit into a whole.

I have studied this word *glory* in this way for almost a year now before putting this into a book. It is my desire to see what the scriptures teach us about this realm so we can have faith for glory to begin to manifest in our lives, the church and the world. This section will include both Old Testament and New Testament scriptures about the glory.

The Glory of God or Glory of Man?

One meaning to the word Glory *is to be held in high esteem.* It is connected to *the value we place on a person to have influence in our lives.* Jesus speaks about glory in this context here.

John 5:44 (NASB)
⁴⁴ "How can you believe, when you receive glory from one another and you do not seek the glory that is from the *one and* only God?

In this season there is going to be a significant push on glory in regard to what or who we esteem highly? The world system, which has a belief that we are fine without God, will have a glory realm. It will look very impressive to many. We need to be careful in regard to what and who we allow to impress us. Whatever impresses us will leave an impression upon us! It is something that would cause a person to devote their entire life to see fulfilled. It is a false glory, but it is very powerful causing men and women to *gain the world while losing their souls.*

Through these intimate encounters with the Father I see how he is breaking off the false glory in which the world wants to wrap society. If we do not know our true identity and acceptance, we will be chasing after the wrong *glory.* Once we know our approval and blessing comes directly from Abba Father, we no longer will seek the fading glory this world system has to offer. Discernment will be essential, because everything called glorious in the hour we are living is not all from the Father.

Kabed is like an anti-glory
In the Old Testament there are two similar sounding words that both have the literal connotation of *being heavy. These are Kabod and Kabed. Kabed* is a word used for glory that is associated with man but never associated with God. When I think about God's glory versus the world's glory this Hebrew word *Kabed* fits into a similar realm. I call this the *anti-glory because of how it affects us.*

Kabed can reflect what happens to man in the realm of this world without the true glory of God. Kabed, like Kabod, is literally interpreted as heavy. Kabed is heavy in a negative sense. It means to be weighed down to the point of not being able to function. Kabod heavy is good while Kabed heavy is not.

In Exodus chapter seventeen we read that the hands of Moses were heavy or *Kabed*. When they were down, Israel would lose the battle taking place in the valley. When he was assisted to hold his hands up Israel would be victorious. There are things going on in our lives every day that try to weigh us down and defeat us. We need God's help for us to lift our hands and move out victoriously!

We also find the word *Kabed,* connected to Moses in Exodus chapter eighteen. He is trying his best to do what God called him to do. But the task for him alone was too *heavy, or Kabed.* Many of us are moving into a season of obeying God and fulfilling our call. There will be times that doing the right thing can be too heavy. We are not tapping into God's glory; we are using our own natural resources and being depleted. This is not sinful, but it can stop us from our destiny.

Right now, many people called into ministry are trying to do God's will out of their own strength, and it is weighing them down. In some cases it is actually creating burn out and depression. This is one reason people get out of ministry. They have nothing left in the tank with which to help people.

I am so thankful that God is restoring joy and strength into these who have had compassion fatigue. They stayed the course, but they were in a dangerous zone where their spiritual batteries were drained. As these have embraced the glory, they are experiencing new vision and strength. They are seeing the glory amplify their ability to operate in the supernatural far greater than ever before!

Even after accessing the true glory to be restored, we must learn to continually access the glory to stay spiritually healthy along the way. *Kabod glory is our new realm of doing ministry with God's ability and strength.*

Kabed, the anti-glory, is also connected to the concept of a person's heart turning hard. Pharaoh's heart was hardened against God in Exodus chapter seven. He saw the miracles but refused to submit to God's plan.

This is a very important time in regards to people coming to faith and walking with God. The glory realm is going to cause people to turn towards God, but it can also be a time when hearts become hard against God. There seems to be less middle ground; people are going to be for God or against him. Those who are against are becoming more vocal and angry. This is because the realm we are living in has shifted.

The goodness of God gives us repentance but each person must make a choice. Guard against strong judgments towards God or man. We must all be very careful that our hearts do not become hard in this hour. People who are believers in Christ can become hard just as those who do not believe in Christ. We must be filled with the Father's love in this hour. It is a love that can overcome the darkness and deception in the atmosphere.

Kabed, speaks about the power of sin in one's life. As gross darkness is covering the earth, we see more and more people weighed down in the bondage and yokes of sin's power. There is more darkness in which to get ensnared now than ever before.

The good news is God promises that *where sin abounds grace abounds the greater.* The glory realm we are walking in has great power to set the captives free. The *Kabod* glory I see being released is going deep into the hearts and souls of people. The love of God is cutting away the chains, healing and restoring lives. I have seen greater deliverance and inner healing in fifteen minutes of uninterrupted Father-time than we used to see in weeks of spiritual help. God's glory is here to set the captives free!

Into the Glory 11

Can We See the Glory?

As I continued my study of the word *glory* I wanted to see real tangible expressions of God at work where he used the word glory to describe his activity. In this way, we can do more than talk about an invisible force that gives us excitement. I want to see what the world we live in will look like when the glory is here with us. This type of glory is the *Kabod*, or the good glory. I found that there are twelve tangible expressions of what *Kabod* glory can look like in the earth.

The first biblical reference to glory is connected to the concept of having a heavy, weighty amount of wealth.

> ### Genesis 31:1 (KJV)
> [1] And he heard the words of Laban's sons, saying, Jacob hath taken away all that was our father's; and of that which was our father's hath he gotten all this glory.
>
> ### Genesis 31:1 (NLT)
> [1] But Jacob soon learned that Laban's sons were grumbling about him. "Jacob has robbed our father of everything!" they said. "He has gained all his wealth at our father's expense."

Kabod often refers to wealth. The covenant between God and Abraham was being extended towards Jacob. He was prospering because of his love for God. The sons of Laban recognized that the great quantity of flocks which Jacob had acquired came at their expense. God moved the glory from Laban to Jacob, and the sons of Laban witnessed the glory shifting. We will see more of this in this coming season.

Using the principle of the first, there is a common thread connecting wealth and God's glory. This is not to say everyone who is rich is prospering because of God's glory on their life or that their motives are pure. I am saying that when we move with humility and proper motives, wealth is a tangible expression of the glory. Many of the promises identified in Isaiah 60 are connected to wealth.

> **Isaiah 60:1-7 (NASB)**
> [1] "Arise, shine; for your light has come, And the glory of the LORD has risen upon you...
> [5] Then thou shalt see, and flow together, and thine heart shall fear, and be enlarged; because the abundance of the sea shall be converted unto thee, the forces of the Gentiles shall come unto thee. [6] The multitude of camels shall cover thee, the dromedaries of Midian and Ephah; all they from Sheba shall come: they shall bring gold and incense; and they shall shew forth the praises of the LORD. [7] All the flocks of Kedar shall be gathered together unto thee, the rams of Nebaioth shall minister unto thee: they shall come up with acceptance on mine altar, and I will glorify the house of my glory.

The wealth to reach the nations is coming in. The wealth to do what God has called you to do is coming in. Don't focus on what you don't have. Put what God has given you to work and let Him multiply, expand and increase the wealth coming during the season of the glory! Agree with this principle at this time with your daily decrees over your wealth coming in to release the glory to the nations!

Three more tangible expressions of glory being in our midst can be found in the life of a man named Eliakim. These three expressions are *a good reputation, to be honored and the ability to hold up under pressure.*

> **Isaiah 22:22-24 (NASB)**
> ²² "Then I will set the key of the house of David on his shoulder, When he opens no one will shut, When he shuts no one will open. ²³ "I will drive him *like* a peg in a firm place, And he will become a throne of glory to his father's house. ²⁴ "So they will hang on him all the glory of his father's house, offspring and issue, all the least of vessels, from bowls to all the jars.

The concept of glory is giving honor to one's family name. God looked upon the evil acts going on and said he was going to put an honorable man in charge. The glory of God is going to uproot evil and place humble, prepared glory carriers into places of honor. We will see a shifting from darkness to light when we see leaders who can carry the glory moved into places of responsibility.

One of our faithful members has become Fire Chief for one of the largest cities in the greater Phoenix area. It was a big step to accept this role. With it came much responsibility. They prayed and asked me to pray with them. After knowing this family for over fifteen years, I have seen how God's hand of glory is resting on this man's life. He is being put into this position of honor for the good of the city and the honorable fire fighters he will lead.

Being a glory carrier is more than praying for people and seeing them fall down. The glory is being released into all seven mountains of society. The way the glory will be revealed needs to make sense to everyone around. People are being promoted because God is promoting them. They have paid a great price of preparation. Now he is wrapping the mantle of glory around them to bring change and greater good to our communities.

Along with honor comes ability to stand up under the pressure. Being in high positions requires much responsibility and accountability. This should never be forgotten or taken lightly. Jesus said *to whom much is given, much is required.*

God's glory will give you the strength to hold up all the weight that will rest on your shoulders. Many will be called to higher positions in this season. You will be given new grace to stand when you say yes to the important task you accept.

One day I was meditating on the word *responsibility*. I felt impressed in my heart from the Lord with this definition. *Responsibility is your response to the ability I have given to you. When you see your ability, and steward it well, I will give you the grace for the new responsibilities you have undertaken.*

In the season of Glory, God is going to be promoting people in all realms of society and at all levels. He will place mantles of glory upon some in the arts, education, entertainment, government, business and more. Families and churches will have mantles of grace to make a difference in our communities as well.

Some of the glory carriers are going to be strong people of faith in Christ, while others will be *pre-believers*. As the glory of God is being released into our communities and the nations, we should not start our checklist with someone's church membership. Remember God looks at the heart. He will be promoting his chosen vessels in arenas of life, because they are the right person for that particular job. Glory carriers of faith need to be ready to pray, support and connect. We never know when a person will come into a personal relationship with Jesus.

Into the Glory — 12

Jesus Promised the Glory

In all my discussions with you in our study about this new season of glory, I have saved the best for last. We, the Church, are entering into this glory season because Jesus promised us that we would see the same glory he was walking in while on the earth. This will be the finest hour of the church age. The glory is what will bring us into a realm of unity and maturity that prepares the bride to meet the bridegroom.

> **John 17:20-23 (NASB)**
> [20] "I do not ask on behalf of these alone, but for those also who believe in Me through their word; [21] that they may all be one; even as You, Father, *are* in Me and I in You, that they also may be in Us, so that the world may believe that You sent Me. [22] "The glory which You have given Me I have given to them, that they may be one, just as We are one; [23] I in them and You in Me, that they may be perfected in unity, so that the world may know that You sent Me, and loved them, even as You have loved Me.

Jesus promised, in what we call his *High Priestly Prayer, the glory you have given me, I have given to them.* This prayer was not simply for the twelve, but for all who would believe in Jesus. Wow! What a promise! Jesus promised that we will access the glory realm.

One reason we are accessing the glory is found in this powerful declaration prayer. *Unity* is the first expression of this glory. The words Jesus used in this prayer show us that this glory is going to *unite us in Christ and the Father*. It is different than being with them. It is moving us into a common shared experience in Christ and the Father that takes us into a new realm of unity with one another.

This realm of unity described by Jesus is *perfected unity*. The Greek word used in this sentence is *teteleiomenoi*. This word means completion or fulfillment. The unity in this glory season is going to bring the Church together in a way to fulfill our mission Jesus gave to us. Jesus had fulfilled his earthly mission through the united glory he shared with Father. Now we are going to finish our mission wrapped in this same *finishing glory!*

The result of our unity through the glory is that *the world may believe that Father sent Jesus*. This is the reason there is a glory season. God wants everyone to know that he sent his Son Jesus. The realm of glory that broke through the darkness on the dusty streets of Palestine is being poured out into our hearts and lives to break the darkness which we are facing in this current world situation.

Jesus walked with a tangible glory upon his life while on the earth, and so will the church. It was the realm where he moved in unity with the Father. He was able to see what Father was doing in heaven, and then he did the same on earth.

> **John 5:19-20 (NASB)**
> [19] Therefore Jesus answered and was saying to them, "Truly, truly, I say to you, the Son can do nothing of Himself, unless *it is* something He sees the Father doing; for whatever the Father does, these things the Son also does in like manner.

> [20] "For the Father loves the Son, and shows Him all things that He Himself is doing; and *the Father* will show Him greater works than these, so that you will marvel.

Being a glory carrier is connected to an intimate relationship with Father that allows us to see what He is doing. There is a price to walk in the glory. We are called to keep our fellowship with the Father pure and clean. It is connected to our obedience and our worship. As we worship, we will see more clearly what the Father has for us to do. As we obey him we will see greater manifestations of the glory. The greatest demonstrations of Father's love will come out of this close, united relationship with the Father.

This is a remarkable thought that many will be able to walk in this realm. Some might say that only Jesus could do such a thing. The truth is Jesus tells us that we will do even greater works because he is with the Father.

> **John 14:11-12 (NASB)**
> [11] "Believe Me that I am in the Father and the Father is in Me; otherwise believe because of the works themselves.
> [12] "Truly, truly, I say to you, he who believes in Me, the works that I do, he will do also; and greater *works* than these he will do; because I go to the Father.

Putting these scriptures together reveals to us a powerful truth of what the glory is really about. It is a relationship of unity with Father like Jesus had. From this realm of unity we move in Father's love and authority to perform mighty works here on earth. Father's love is being lavished upon many in our day and hour. It is here in our world that many will believe that the Father sent Jesus for them to know and experience eternal life.

The glory is a realm we all are called to experience. It is a realm that will change everyone's life.

John 1:14 (KJV)
¹⁴ And the Word was made flesh, and dwelt among us, (and we beheld his glory, the glory as of the only begotten of the Father,) full of grace and truth.

John wrote in the beginning of his gospel that *we beheld his glory. Beheld is defined as a careful, intense observation which creates a sense of wonder.*

The glory of Jesus was a tangible expression that could be touched, felt or experienced. This shows us that people are affected by encountering the glory. This glory is something Christ brought with him from heaven when he came to the earth. It was manifested by the words he spoke, the love he gave and the power released in miracles.

Just as the disciples learned about the glory from Jesus so now this new move of glory is starting within the Church. We are learning to gather in new ways and worship in new ways. This is how God is going to cause us to shine seven times brighter than when we began. It is from these new encounters that we will be going out from the Church. Get ready to see the church looking really different. Expect new expressions of God's love to be released in new ways.

The first manifestation of the glory in the life of Jesus was to prepare disciples to be believers. The glory began with Jesus in his first miracle performed at the wedding in Cana.

John 2:11 (NASB)
¹¹ This beginning of *His* signs Jesus did in Cana of Galilee, and manifested His glory, and His disciples believed in Him.

Father is once again doing great miracles in us, because they will start flowing through us. We are now entering into a time when seeing miracles becomes normal. We should always be in awe of God and give him praise for all he does. In this time we are going to be giving him a lot of praise, because the glory carriers are going to be seeing consistent demonstrations of signs and wonders wherever we go!

In the past season when Holy Spirit was being emphasized, the church was learning to move in spiritual gifts. Paul called spiritual gifts, *manifestations of the Spirit. (Ref. 1 Corinthians 12:7)* Now the Church is going to move into *manifestations of the glory!* This is going to be like spiritual gifts on steroids.

The glory is different than spiritual gifts. Many different ministers and leaders who have been baptized into the glory have been reporting that everything they have done in the past is much stronger. They have been moving in the gifts of the Spirit for many years and been very fruitful. Now in this new season of glory, their *gifts seem to be multiplied and amplified.* We are now seeing the *manifestations of the glory.*

The glory represents what heaven is like. The glory demonstrated on the earth is the same glory that existed with the Father before the world as we know it began.

> **John 17:5 (NASB)**
> ⁵ "Now, Father, glorify Me together with Yourself, with the glory which I had with You before the world was.

This is the glory which created the heavens and the earth. It is the realm which releases creative miracles, ideas, solutions and impartation of power beyond the limits of the natural world. The glory realm is a place where we are not restricted by the natural or the impossible.

I am aware when this level of glory is present. It comes through unity and intense love. It hits me in worship and prepares me to move beyond the forces which try to limit me. There is a costly requirement to remain in this realm. We must have love for one another. All judgments and evil thoughts about each other must be surrendered. We cannot carry these into the glory. The fullness of unity between the Father and the Son is what is required for us to reach into the realm of glory which Jesus walked in while on the earth.

> **John 17:24 (NASB)**
> ²⁴ "Father, I desire that they also, whom You have given Me, be with Me where I am, so that they may see My glory which You have given Me, for You loved Me before the foundation of the world.

Jesus really loves people. We can read about love and talk about love, but when we are in the glory, we see people with this love. We must guard our hearts from the forces which try to destroy our love relationships. This will allows us to see each other through His eyes. The love released in the glory will attract people to us like they were attracted to Jesus.

Jesus prayed for us to know this realm of glory. It is possible to attain. It is a realm that the church once knew and now is being restored to us again. Here in this place we are experiencing Father's love, acceptance and approval. It is here that the works of Jesus become a regular part of our daily lives.

Have you ever felt there was more to your walk with God than you are currently experiencing? Have you ever wondered if it was possible to love like Jesus loved? Have you ever desired to know Father's heart be empowered to do what he desired you to do on a daily basis?

The new season of the Father's glory is where these questions are answered. It is a place where we are invited to go and see our lives changed forever. Right now I invite you to do what we have been doing every Monday night when we gather. Close your eyes and put out both hands together like you are expecting Father to put something into your hands. As you start saying this prayer you are going to feel the glory river starting to flow over you. Soon you will be washed deeper and deeper into his glory realm. As you say this simple prayer with me get ready for your life to change forever.

> *Father, fill my life with your glory. Wash over me with your waves of glory until I am changed. Free me from every curse which would hold me back from all that you have in store for me as my inheritance. Fill me now with your amazing love, acceptance and peace. Take me into your glory. Make me a Glory Carrier.*

About the Author

Greg Brown is the apostolic leader of Skyway Apostolic Center and ASCEND International. He is married to Dawn, and they have two married adult children. Pastors Greg and Dawn first arrived at Skyway Church in 1983 to serve as the Youth Ministers. In 1989, they started leading Skyway with 65 members. In 2004, Skyway Church built their new sanctuary with a 25-acre campus in Goodyear, Arizona. The church currently reaches over 1,500 and has multiple pastors on staff. Greg Brown is the apostle over ASCEND International, which represents over 70,000 believers, over 15,000 ministries and churches, and more than 30 commissioned ministry leaders across 20 nations.

Greg graduated from Grand Canyon University in 1986 with his bachelor's degree. He earned his Wagner Leadership Institute Doctorate in Practical Ministry in 2010 and currently serves as the chancellor of WLI Phoenix. He has authored two previous books, *Navigating the Crisis* and *The 7 Laws of Breakthrough*.

If interested in hosting Greg Brown as a guest speaker, please send your requests to info@skywaychurch.com or call 623-935-4858.

Into the Glory

Made in the USA
Middletown, DE
03 April 2016